Taste of Home
Soups, Stews
& more

TASTE OF HOME BOOKS • RDA ENTHUSIAST BRANDS, LLC • MILWAUKEE, WI

ISBN: 978-1-61765-999-7
LOCC: 2020940119
Component Number: 116700102H

Executive Editor: Mark Hagen
Senior Art Director: Raeann Thompson
Assistant Art Director: Courtney Lovetere
Senior Designer: Sophie Beck
Designer: Jazmin Delgado
Copy Editor: Sara Strauss
Contributing Editor: Michelle Rozumalski

Cover:
Photographer: Dan Roberts
Set Stylist: Stacey Genaw
Food Stylist: Josh Rink

Pictured on front cover:
Spinach & Tortellini Soup, p. 72; Tex-Mex Chili, p. 44;
Broccoli Beer Cheese Soup, p. 32

Pictured on title page:
Slow-Cooker Quinoa Chili, p. 47

Pictured on back cover:
Chickpea Tortilla Soup, p. 26; The Ultimate Chicken
Noodle Soup, p. 17; Steak & Beer Chili, p. 46

INSTANT POT is a trademark of Double Insight Inc.
This publication has not been authorized, sponsored
or otherwise approved by Double Insight Inc.

Printed in Malaysia
1 3 5 7 9 10 8 6 4 2

P. 97

P. 9

P. 41

P. 74

It's time to indulge in the comfort of a warm bowl of soup. Nothing brightens cloudy days, delivers goodness or warms hearts quicker than a savory broth featuring herbs, vegetables, beans or pasta.

The editors of *Taste of Home* grouped their favorite soups together for **Soups, Stews & More,** a must-have cookbook that today's family cooks have been wanting. Inside you'll find 140 of the sensational delights you most depend on when the temperature drops. From Mom's best chicken soup and Dad's five-alarm chili to impressive chowders and decadent bisques, the ideal dish is always at your fingertips with this new collection.

For the ultimate stick-to-your-ribs specialties, see the Cheesy & Creamy chapter or turn to the Heartiest Stews section for fantastic meal-in-one options. Page to the Chilis area when the gang is headed over to watch the big game, or check out the recipes in the Healthy & Light chapter when you want to trim down. Not sure what to make for dinner? Revisit a staple with the All-Time Classics section or see Cook It Fast or Slow for recipes that can be made in either a slow cooker or an Instant Pot. You choose!

You'll also enjoy...

- A no-fuss guide to making homemade broth and stock

- Dozens of tips, hints and secrets to speed dinner prep

- Vegetarian and meatless recipes, as well as seafood greats

- A complete set of nutrition facts with every dish

Plus, at-a-glance icons make meal planning a snap...

🕐 Fast-fix dishes are ready in just 30 minutes.

5i 5-ingredient soups call for just a few staples, not including salt, pepper, water, oils or optional items such as garnishes.

❄ Freeze these for now and reheat them on a busy night. Reheating directions included.

🍲 Slow-cooker recipes simmer on their own.

🍲 Instant Pot items come together quickly in your electric pressure cooker.

You'll also find prep/cook times with each recipe, step-by-step directions, more than 150 photos, and diabetic exchanges where applicable. Simply flip through this lovely book and see how easy it'd be to ladle out bowls of joy tonight. With **Soups, Stews & More,** homemade comfort is always the special of the day.

Contents

P. 64

P. 11

More ways to connect with us: 📘 🐦 📷 📌

SHOPTASTEOFHOME.COM

Stock Up!

Making your own broth from scratch is easier than you think, and it's the simplest way to take your soups and stews to the next level. Simmer these three staples to start your stash.

HOW TO MAKE
VEGETABLE BROTH

Use this homemade broth in any recipe that calls for vegetable broth. It's an easy alternative to store-bought versions, and it'll be lower in sodium as well. Cover and refrigerate the broth up to three days or freeze up to six months.

1 cup: 148 cal., 6g fat (1g sat. fat), 0 chol., 521mg sod., 22g carb. (9g sugars, 5g fiber), 4g pro.

💬 TIP

Avoid seasoning your broth with herbs and spices. The long simmer time extracts a lot of flavor from the herbs, which might overpower the finished broth. You'll add herbs and spices when you use the broth in a recipe.

Prep: 45 min. • **Cook:** 1¾ hours • **Makes:** 5½ cups

2 Tbsp. olive oil	3 medium carrots, cut into 1-in. pieces
2 medium onions, cut into wedges	8 cups water
2 celery ribs, cut into 1-in. pieces	½ lb. fresh mushrooms, quartered
1 whole garlic bulb, separated into cloves and peeled	1 cup packed fresh parsley sprigs
3 medium leeks, white and light green parts only, cleaned and cut into 1-in. pieces	4 sprigs fresh thyme
	1 tsp. salt
	½ tsp. whole peppercorns
	1 bay leaf

1. Heat oil in a stockpot over medium heat until hot. Add onions, celery and garlic. Cook and stir 5 minutes or until vegetables are tender. Add leeks and carrots; cook and stir 5 minutes.

2. Add water, mushrooms, parsley, thyme, salt, peppercorns and bay leaf; bring to a boil. Reduce heat; simmer, uncovered, 1 hour.

3. Remove from heat. Strain through a cheesecloth-lined colander; discard vegetables. If using immediately, skim fat. Or refrigerate 8 hours or overnight; remove fat from surface before using.

HOW TO MAKE
CHICKEN BROTH

Make this classic recipe your go-to in dishes that call for chicken stock. Collagen-rich and laced with veggies and herbs, homemade is healthier than commercial versions, which can be laden with preservatives and salt. This broth will keep in the fridge, tightly covered, for four to five days. Or seal it tightly in a freezer-safe container and freeze it for up to a year.

Prep: 10 min. • **Cook:** 3¼ hours + chilling • **Makes:** about 6 cups

2½ lbs. bony chicken pieces (legs, wings, necks or back bones)	quartered
	2 bay leaves
2 celery ribs with leaves, cut into chunks	½ tsp. dried rosemary, crushed
2 medium carrots, cut into chunks	½ tsp. dried thyme
	8 to 10 whole peppercorns
2 medium onions,	2 qt. cold water

1 cup: 245 cal., 14g fat (4g sat. fat), 61mg chol., 80mg sod., 3g carb. (4g sugars, 2g fiber), 21g pro.

1. Place all ingredients in a soup kettle or Dutch oven. Slowly bring to a boil; reduce the heat until the mixture is at just a simmer.

2. Simmer, uncovered, for 3-4 hours, skimming foam as necessary.

3. Set chicken aside until cool enough to handle. Remove meat from bones. Discard bones; save meat for another use. Strain broth, discarding vegetables and seasonings.

4. Refrigerate for 8 hours or overnight. Skim fat from surface.

1 cup: 30 cal., 0 fat (0 sat. fat), 0 chol., 75mg sod., 0 carb. (0 sugars, 0 fiber), 6g pro.

HOW TO MAKE
BONE BROTH

Whether you're adding it to soups or sipping it straight, this rich stock is well worth the effort. You'll want to simmer it for 8-24 hours, so we recommend making it a weekend project. Measure some into your favorite soup recipe now, then freeze the rest for up to six months.

Prep: 1½ hours • **Cook:** 8-24 hours
Makes: about 2½ qt.

- 4 lbs. meaty beef soup bones (beef shanks or short ribs)
- 2 medium onions, quartered
- 3 chopped medium carrots, optional
- ½ cup warm water (110° to 115°)
- 3 bay leaves
- 3 garlic cloves
- 8 to 10 whole peppercorns
  Cold water

1. Place bones in a large stockpot or Dutch oven; add enough water to cover. Bring to a boil over medium-high heat; reduce heat and simmer 15 minutes. Drain, discarding liquid. Rinse bones; drain.

2. Meanwhile, preheat oven to 450°. In a large roasting pan, roast boiled bones, uncovered, 30 minutes. Add quartered onions and, if desired, chopped carrots. Roast until bones and vegetables are dark brown, 30-45 minutes longer; drain fat.

3. Transfer bones and vegetables to a large stockpot or Dutch oven.

4. Add ½ cup warm water to the roasting pan; stir to loosen browned bits. Transfer pan juices to pot. Add seasonings and enough cold water just to cover. Slowly bring to a boil, about 30 minutes. Reduce the heat; simmer, covered with the lid slightly ajar, 8-24 hours, skimming foam. If necessary, add water as needed to keep ingredients covered.

5. Remove beef bones; cool. Strain the broth through a cheesecloth-lined colander, discarding the vegetables and seasonings.

 TIP

The longer you simmer the broth, the more collagen will be extracted from the bones. This component gives the final broth a silky, smooth texture and body. Don't worry if the bones start to fall apart or crumble. This is a sign you've extracted as much as you can from them.

6. If using immediately, skim fat. Or refrigerate broth 8 hours or overnight; remove the fat from the surface.

SOUP-FREEZING TIPS

Keep this expert advice in mind so your soup tastes just as good as it did the day you made it.

1. Avoid freezing soups with pasta, rice or pieces of potato. These starches soak up liquid and get soggy when reheated. Pureed potatoes, though, hold up well. If you need to freeze one of these soups, hold the pasta, rice or potato pieces. Add them after you've thawed the soup.

2. Omit the dairy, too. A freezer does odd things to milk's texture, and the soup will be grainy when it thaws. It's best to add milk and other dairy products when you're reheating the thawed soup.

3. Never freeze hot soup. If you do, it will develop large ice crystals and freeze unevenly, translating to mushy soup when you thaw it. For best freezing results, cool your soup to at least room temperature (but, preferably, below 40° in the refrigerator) to help it freeze faster and better.

4. Watch portion size. Freezing your soup in one- or two-person portions makes for easy meal planning, and it also helps the soup freeze faster.

5. Opt for freezer-safe containers and leave about 1½ inches of headspace. Soup will expand as it freezes, and you don't want your container to crack or break. When you're ready to eat, run cold water over the outside of the container to loosen the soup. It will pop right out into your pot.

THE ULTIMATE CHICKEN
NOODLE SOUP, P. 17

All-Time Classics

Soup and stew lovers just keep going back to these traditional, time-honored favorites.

FENNEL CARROT
SOUP, P. 13

Seafood Gumbo

Gumbo is one of the reasons Louisiana cuisine is world famous. We live across the border in Texas and just can't get enough of this traditional Cajun dish featuring okra, shrimp, spicy seasonings and what is called the holy trinity—onions, green peppers and celery. If you prefer, replace the seafood with chicken, duck or sausage.
—*Ruth Aubey, San Antonio, TX*

Prep: 20 min. • **Cook:** 30 min.
Makes: 24 servings

- 1 cup all-purpose flour
- 1 cup canola oil
- 4 cups chopped onion
- 2 cups chopped celery
- 2 cups chopped green pepper
- 1 cup sliced green onions
- 4 cups chicken broth
- 8 cups water
- 4 cups sliced okra
- 2 Tbsp. paprika
- 1 Tbsp. salt
- 2 tsp. oregano
- 1 tsp. ground black pepper
- 6 cups small shrimp, rinsed and drained, or seafood of your choice
- 1 cup minced fresh parsley
- 2 Tbsp. Cajun seasoning

1. In a heavy Dutch oven, combine flour and oil until smooth. Cook over medium-high heat for 5 minutes, stirring constantly. Reduce the heat to medium. Cook and stir about 10 minutes more or until the mixture is reddish brown.
2. Add the onion, celery, green pepper and green onions; cook and stir for 5 minutes. Add the broth, water, okra, paprika, salt, oregano and pepper. Bring to boil; reduce heat and simmer, covered, for 10 minutes.
3. Add the shrimp and parsley. Simmer, uncovered, about 5 minutes more or until the seafood is done. Remove from heat; stir in Cajun seasoning.
1 cup: 166 cal., 10g fat (1g sat. fat), 96mg chol., 900mg sod., 10g carb. (2g sugars, 2g fiber), 10g pro.

Weeknight Goulash

With a little help from your slow cooker, you can put in a full day's work, run some errands and still prepare dinner for your family. This meaty goulash is delicious over egg noodles or spaetzle.
—*Cyndy Gerken, Naples, FL*

Prep: 25 min. • **Cook:** 8½ hours
Makes: 2 servings

- 1 lb. beef stew meat
- 1 Tbsp. olive oil
- 1 cup beef broth
- 1 small onion, chopped
- ¼ cup ketchup
- 1 Tbsp. Worcestershire sauce
- 1½ tsp. brown sugar
- 1½ tsp. paprika
- ¼ tsp. ground mustard
- 1 Tbsp. all-purpose flour
- 2 Tbsp. water
  Hot cooked egg noodles or spaetzle

1. In a large skillet, brown beef in oil; drain. Transfer to a 1½-qt. slow cooker. Combine the broth, onion, ketchup, Worcestershire sauce, brown sugar, paprika and mustard. Pour over beef. Cover and cook on low until meat is tender, 8-10 hours.
2. In a small bowl, combine the flour and water until smooth. Gradually stir into the beef mixture. Cover and cook on high until thickened, about 30 minutes longer. Serve with noodles.
1 cup: 478 cal., 23g fat (7g sat. fat), 141mg chol., 1005mg sod., 20g carb. (14g sugars, 1g fiber), 45g pro.

SEAFOOD GUMBO

CHICKEN MATZO BALL SOUP

4. In another stockpot, bring water to a boil. Drop rounded tablespoonfuls of matzo ball dough into boiling water. Reduce heat; cover and simmer until a toothpick inserted into a matzo ball comes out clean (do not lift cover while simmering), 20-25 minutes.
5. Carefully remove matzo balls from water with a slotted spoon; place 1 matzo ball in each soup bowl. Add soup.
1 cup: 167 cal., 10g fat (2g sat. fat), 60mg chol., 523mg sod., 8g carb. (1g sugars, 1g fiber), 11g pro.

Hearty Beef Barley Soup
Here's classic comfort food by the bowlful! My whole family loves the chunks of tender beef combined with sliced carrots, fresh mushrooms and quick-cooking barley.
—*Barbara Beattie, Glen Allen, VA*

- -

Prep: 10 min. • **Cook:** 30 min.
Makes: 4 servings

    2   Tbsp. all-purpose flour
    ½   tsp. salt
    ¼   tsp. pepper, divided
    1   lb. lean beef top sirloin steak, cut into
        ½-in. cubes
    1   Tbsp. canola oil
    2   cups sliced fresh mushrooms
    2   cans (14½ oz. each) reduced-sodium
        beef broth
    2   medium carrots, sliced
    ¼   tsp. garlic powder
    ¼   tsp. dried thyme
    ½   cup quick-cooking barley

1. In a shallow dish, combine the flour, salt and ⅛ tsp. pepper. Add the beef and turn to coat. In a Dutch oven, brown beef in oil over medium heat until the meat is no longer pink. Remove beef and set aside.
2. In the same pan, saute mushrooms until tender. Add the beef broth, carrots, garlic powder, thyme and remaining pepper; bring to a boil. Add barley and beef. Reduce heat; cover and simmer for 20-25 minutes or until the meat, vegetables and barley are tender.
1¼ cups: 306 cal., 9g fat (2g sat. fat), 50mg chol., 748mg sod., 25g carb. (3g sugars, 5g fiber), 31g pro. **Diabetic exchanges:** 3 lean meat, 1½ starch, 1 vegetable, ½ fat.

Chicken Matzo Ball Soup
I think the keys to this amazing soup are slow-cooking it and using boxed matzo ball mix. Some people swear by using seltzer, but I find it's not necessary—the mix makes perfect, fluffy matzo balls every time thanks to its baking powder. Add chicken fat (schmaltz) for extra-authentic flavor. The matzo balls will taste as if they came straight from Grandma's kitchen!
—*Shannon Sarna, South Orange, NJ*

- -

Prep: 30 min. + chilling
Cook: 1½ hours
Makes: 26 servings

    1   broiler/fryer chicken (3 to 4 lbs.)
    1   lb. chicken wings
    6   qt. water
    3   large carrots, chopped
    2   medium parsnips, peeled
         and chopped
    1   medium turnip, peeled and chopped
    1   large onion, chopped
    1   bunch fresh dill sprigs
    1   bunch fresh parsley sprigs
    1½   tsp. whole peppercorns
    3   tsp. salt

MATZO BALLS
    1   pkg. (5 oz.) matzo ball mix
    4   large eggs
    ¼   cup safflower oil
    ¼   cup rendered chicken fat
    2   Tbsp. snipped fresh dill
    2   Tbsp. minced fresh parsley
    10   cups water

1. Place chicken and wings in a stockpot; add the water, vegetables, herbs and seasonings. Slowly bring to a boil. Reduce heat; simmer, covered, 1-2 hours.
2. Remove chicken and wings and cool. Strain broth through a cheesecloth-lined colander; reserve vegetables. Skim fat. Remove meat from bones and cut into bite-sized pieces; discard bones. Return broth, vegetables and meat to the pot. If using immediately, skim fat. Or cool the broth, then refrigerate 8 hours or overnight; remove fat from surface before using. (Broth may be refrigerated up to 3 days or frozen 4-6 months.)
3. Meanwhile, in a large bowl, beat the matzo ball mix, eggs, oil, chicken fat, dill and parsley until combined. Cover and refrigerate for at least 30 minutes.

The Best Ever Tomato Soup

Creamy, rich and bursting with brightness, this is the ultimate sidekick to grilled cheese and is super all by itself, too. See if you agree!
—*Josh Rink, Milwaukee, WI*

- -

Prep: 20 min. • **Cook:** 30 min.
Makes: 16 servings

- 3 Tbsp. olive oil
- 3 Tbsp. butter
- ¼ to ½ tsp. crushed red pepper flakes
- 3 large carrots, peeled and chopped
- 1 large onion, chopped
- 2 garlic cloves, minced
- 2 tsp. dried basil
- 3 cans (28 oz. each) whole peeled tomatoes
- 1 container (32 oz.) chicken stock
- 2 Tbsp. tomato paste
- 3 tsp. sugar
- 1 tsp. salt
- ½ tsp. pepper
- 1 cup heavy whipping cream, optional
  Fresh basil leaves, thinly sliced, optional

1. In a 6-qt. stockpot or Dutch oven, heat oil, butter and pepper flakes over medium heat until butter is melted. Add carrots and onion; cook, uncovered, over medium heat, stirring frequently, until the vegetables are softened, 8-10 minutes. Add garlic and dried basil; cook and stir 1 minute longer. Stir in tomatoes, chicken stock, tomato paste, sugar, salt and pepper; mix well. Bring to a boil. Reduce heat; simmer, uncovered, to let the flavors blend, 20-25 minutes.

2. Remove pan from heat. Using a blender, puree the soup in batches until smooth. If desired, slowly stir in heavy cream, stirring continuously to incorporate; return to the stove to heat through. Top servings with fresh basil if desired.

1 cup: 104 cal., 5g fat (2g sat. fat), 6mg chol., 572mg sod., 15g carb. (10g sugars, 2g fiber), 3g pro. **Diabetic exchanges:** 1 starch, 1 fat.

TIP

Versatile tomato soup gives you the perfect opportunity to get creative with toppings. We garnished this recipe with sliced fresh basil, but feel free to dollop on sour cream, add small cubes of cream cheese or even spoon on a little of last night's taco meat.

THE BEST EVER
TOMATO SOUP

CHUNKY CREAMY
CHICKEN SOUP

Chunky Creamy Chicken Soup

I'm a stay-at-home mom who relies on my slow cooker for fast, nutritious meals with minimal prep and cleanup. When I tried a new chicken soup recipe, I knew it was a keeper because I didn't have leftovers and my husband asked for it again.
—*Nancy Clow, Mallorytown, ON*

Prep: 15 min. • **Cook:** 4½ hours
Makes: 7 servings

- 1½ lbs. boneless skinless chicken breasts, cut into 2-in. strips
- 2 tsp. canola oil
- ⅔ cup finely chopped onion
- 2 medium carrots, chopped
- 2 celery ribs, chopped
- 1 cup frozen corn
- 2 cans (10¾ oz. each) condensed cream of potato soup, undiluted
- 1½ cups chicken broth
- 1 tsp. dill weed
- 1 cup frozen peas
- ½ cup half-and-half cream

1. In a large skillet over medium-high heat, brown chicken in oil. Transfer to a 5-qt. slow cooker; add onion, carrots, celery and corn.
2. In a large bowl, whisk cream of potato soup, chicken broth and dill until blended; stir into slow cooker. Cover and cook on low until chicken and vegetables are tender, about 4 hours .
3. Stir in the peas and half-and-half cream. Cover and cook until heated through, about 30 minutes longer.
1 cup: 229 cal., 7g fat (3g sat. fat), 66mg chol., 629mg sod., 17g carb. (5g sugars, 3g fiber), 24g pro.

Hearty Navy Bean Soup

Bean soup is a family favorite that I make often. Use economical dried beans and a ham hock to create this comforting classic.
—*Mildred Lewis, Temple, TX*

- -

Prep: 30 min. + soaking • **Cook:** 1¾ hours
Makes: 10 servings

- 3 cups (1½ lbs.) dried navy beans
- 1 can (14½ oz.) diced tomatoes, undrained
- 1 large onion, chopped
- 1 meaty ham hock or 1 cup diced cooked ham
- 2 cups chicken broth
- 2½ cups water
  Salt and pepper to taste
  Minced fresh parsley

1. Rinse and sort the beans; soak according to package directions.
2. Drain and rinse beans, discarding liquid. Place in a Dutch oven. Add the tomatoes with juice, onion, ham hock, broth, water, salt and pepper. Bring to a boil. Reduce heat; cover and simmer until beans are tender, about 1½ hours.
3. Add more water if necessary. Remove ham hock and let it stand until cool enough to handle. Remove meat from bone; discard bone. Cut meat into bite-sized pieces; set aside. (For a thicker soup, cool slightly, then puree beans in a food processor or blender and return to pan.) Return ham to soup and heat through. Garnish with parsley.

1 cup: 245 cal., 2g fat (0 sat. fat), 8mg chol., 352mg sod., 42g carb. (5g sugars, 16g fiber), 18g pro. **Diabetic exchanges:** 3 starch, 2 lean meat.

PASTA FAGIOLI SOUP

Pasta Fagioli Soup

My husband likes my version of this soup so much that he no longer eats it at restaurants. He'd rather savor the one we can have at home! The recipe is so easy to make and is hearty enough to be a complete dinner.
—*Brenda Thomas, Springfield, MO*

- -

Takes: 30 min.
Makes: 5 servings

- ½ lb. Italian turkey sausage links, casings removed, crumbled
- 1 small onion, chopped
- 1½ tsp. canola oil
- 1 garlic clove, minced
- 2 cups water
- 1 can (15½ oz.) great northern beans, rinsed and drained
- 1 can (14½ oz.) diced tomatoes, undrained
- 1 can (14½ oz.) reduced-sodium chicken broth
- ¾ cup uncooked elbow macaroni
- ¼ tsp. pepper
- 1 cup fresh spinach leaves, cut as desired
- 5 tsp. shredded Parmesan cheese

1. In a large saucepan, cook sausage over medium heat until no longer pink; drain, remove from pan and set aside. In the same pan, saute onion in oil until tender. Add garlic; saute 1 minute longer.
2. Add the water, beans, tomatoes, chicken broth, macaroni and pepper; bring to a boil. Cook, uncovered, until macaroni is tender, 8-10 minutes.
3. Reduce heat to low; stir in the sausage and spinach. Cook until spinach is wilted, 2-3 minutes. Garnish with cheese.

1⅓ cups: 228 cal., 7g fat (1g sat. fat), 29mg chol., 841mg sod., 27g carb. (4g sugars, 6g fiber), 16g pro. **Diabetic exchanges:** 1½ starch, 1 lean meat, 1 vegetable, ½ fat.

Fennel Carrot Soup

Here's a wonderful first course for Christmas dinner or a special treat anytime. The curry and fennel seed really complement the carrots, apple and sweet potato.
—*Marlene Bursey, Waverly, NS*

Prep: 10 min. • **Cook:** 45 min.
Makes: 8 servings

- 1 Tbsp. butter
- ½ tsp. fennel seed
- 1½ lbs. carrots, sliced
- 1 medium sweet potato, peeled and cubed
- 1 medium apple, peeled and cubed
- 3 cans (14½ oz. each) vegetable broth
- 2 Tbsp. uncooked long grain rice
- 1 bay leaf
- ¼ tsp. curry powder
- 1 Tbsp. lemon juice
- ½ tsp. salt
- ¼ tsp. white pepper
- 2 Tbsp. minced fresh parsley

1. In a large saucepan, melt the butter over medium-high heat. Add the fennel; cook and stir 2-3 minutes or until lightly toasted. Add carrots, sweet potato and apple; cook and stir 5 minutes longer.
2. Stir in vegetable broth, rice, bay leaf and curry powder; bring to a boil. Reduce heat; simmer, covered, 30 minutes or until the vegetables and rice are soft.
3. Remove from heat; cool slightly. Discard bay leaf. Process in batches in a blender until smooth; return to pan. Stir in lemon juice, salt and pepper. Cook over medium heat 5 minutes or until heated through, stirring occasionally. Sprinkle with parsley.
1 cup: 117 cal., 2g fat (1g sat. fat), 4mg chol., 989mg sod., 23g carb. (0 sugars, 3g fiber), 3g pro. **Diabetic exchanges:** 2 vegetable, 1 starch.

Cheese Soup with a Twist

One of my favorite childhood memories is of my Aunt Claire ladling up bowls of her famous soup. Her "twist" was the addition of olives. She served slices of warm buttered bread on the side for a down-home lunch. Now I love making it myself to share.
—*Rob Feezor, Alexandria, VA*

Takes: 30 min. • **Makes:** 8 servings

- 5 bacon strips, diced
- ½ cup chopped celery
- ½ cup chopped onion
- ½ cup chopped green pepper
- ¼ cup all-purpose flour
- ¼ tsp. coarsely ground pepper
- 4 cups reduced-sodium chicken broth
- 2 cups whole milk
- 3 cups cubed Velveeta
- ½ cup sliced pimiento-stuffed olives
- ½ cup grated carrots
- 2 Tbsp. sherry, optional
  Minced fresh parsley

1. In a Dutch oven, cook the bacon over medium heat until crisp. Using a slotted spoon, remove to paper towels to drain. In the drippings, saute celery, onion and green pepper until tender.
2. Stir in the flour and pepper until blended; gradually add the chicken broth and milk. Bring to a boil; cook and stir for 1-2 minutes or until thickened.
3. Add cheese, olives, carrots and, if desired, sherry; cook and stir until cheese is melted. Sprinkle servings with parsley and bacon.
1 cup: 292 cal., 21g fat (10g sat. fat), 50mg chol., 1155mg sod., 13g carb. (8g sugars, 1g fiber), 14g pro.

FENNEL CARROT SOUP

CLASSIC FRENCH ONION SOUP

Easy Butternut Squash Soup

When the weather turns cool, you'll make everyone feel cozy with this fall-flavored recipe. The cream adds richness, but if you're looking to cut calories, simply leave it out.
—Taste of Home *Test Kitchen*

Takes: 30 min. • **Makes:** 9 servings

- 1 Tbsp. olive oil
- 1 large onion, chopped
- 3 garlic cloves, minced
- 1 medium butternut squash (3 lbs.), peeled and cubed
- 4 cups vegetable broth
- ¾ tsp. salt
- ¼ tsp. pepper
- ½ cup heavy whipping cream
  Optional: Additional heavy whipping cream and crispy sage leaves

1. In a large saucepan, heat oil over medium heat. Add onion; cook and stir until tender. Add garlic; cook 1 minute longer.
2. Stir in squash, vegetable broth, salt and pepper; bring to a boil. Reduce heat; simmer, covered, 10-15 minutes or until the squash is tender. Puree soup using an immersion blender. Or cool slightly and puree soup in batches in a blender; return to the pan. Add the cream; cook and stir until heated through. If desired, garnish with additional heavy whipping cream and crispy sage.
1 cup: 157 cal., 7g fat (4g sat. fat), 17mg chol., 483mg sod., 23g carb. (6g sugars, 6g fiber), 3g pro.

 TIP

Love the creamy comfort of this soup but want something a bit heartier? Bulk up your bowlful by stirring in some cooked rice.

Classic French Onion Soup

For a special treat, enjoy your French onion soup the same way my granddaughter Becky does. I serve it to her in a French onion soup bowl complete with garlic croutons and gobs of melted Swiss cheese on top.
—Lou Sansevero, Ferron, UT

Prep: 20 min. • **Cook:** 2 hours
Makes: 12 servings

- 5 Tbsp. olive oil, divided
- 1 Tbsp. butter
- 8 cups thinly sliced onions (about 3 lbs.)
- 3 garlic cloves, minced
- ½ cup port wine
- 2 cartons (32 oz. each) beef broth
- ½ tsp. pepper
- ¼ tsp. salt
- 24 slices French bread baguette (½ in. thick)
- 2 large garlic cloves, peeled and halved
- ¾ cup shredded Gruyere or Swiss cheese

1. In a Dutch oven, heat 2 Tbsp. oil and butter over medium heat. Add the onions; cook and stir until softened, 10-13 minutes. Reduce heat to medium-low; cook, stirring occasionally, until deep golden brown, 30-40 minutes. Add minced garlic; cook 2 minutes longer.
2. Stir in wine. Bring to a boil; cook until liquid is reduced by half. Add beef broth, pepper and salt; return to a boil. Reduce heat. Simmer, covered, stirring occasionally, for 1 hour.
3. Meanwhile, preheat oven to 400°. Place baguette slices on a baking sheet; brush both sides with remaining oil. Bake until toasted, 3-5 minutes on each side. Rub toasts with halved garlic.
4. To serve, place twelve 8-oz. broiler-safe bowls or ramekins on baking sheets; place 2 toasts in each. Ladle with soup; top with cheese. Broil 4 in. from heat until cheese is melted.
¾ cup soup with 1 slice bread and 1 Tbsp. cheese: 172 cal., 9g fat (3g sat. fat), 10mg chol., 773mg sod., 16g carb. (3g sugars, 1g fiber), 6g pro.

EASY BUTTERNUT
SQUASH SOUP

Cream of Turkey & Wild Rice Soup

A dear friend brought me this when I was ill. It was so warming and comforting, I asked for the recipe. Now when friends aren't feeling well, I bring them the same meal.
—Doris Cox, New Freedom, PA

Prep: 15 min. • **Cook:** 20 min.
Makes: 6 servings

- 1 medium onion, chopped
- 1 can (4 oz.) sliced mushrooms, drained
- 2 Tbsp. butter
- 3 cups water
- 2 cups chicken broth
- 1 pkg. (6 oz.) long grain and wild rice mix
- 2 cups diced cooked turkey
- 1 cup heavy whipping cream
  Minced fresh parsley

In a large saucepan, saute the onion and mushrooms in butter until onion is tender. Add the water, broth and rice mix with seasoning; bring to a boil. Reduce heat; simmer for 20-25 minutes or until the rice is tender. Stir in turkey and cream; heat through. Sprinkle with parsley.
1 cup: 364 cal., 21g fat (12g sat. fat), 100mg chol., 857mg sod., 25g carb. (3g sugars, 1g fiber), 19g pro.

Beef Vegetable Soup

Here's a hearty, family-pleasing dinner in a bowl. I love the convenience of doing all the prep in the morning, then letting my slow cooker do the rest of the work.
—Jean Hutzell, Dubuque, IA

Prep: 20 min. • **Cook:** 9 hours
Makes: 7 servings

- 1 lb. lean ground beef (90% lean)
- 1 medium onion, chopped
- ½ tsp. salt
- ¼ tsp. pepper
- 3 cups water
- 3 medium potatoes, peeled and cut into ¾-in. cubes
- 1 can (14½ oz.) Italian diced tomatoes, undrained
- 1 can (11½ oz.) V8 juice
- 1 cup chopped celery
- 1 cup sliced carrots
- 2 Tbsp. sugar
- 1 Tbsp. dried parsley flakes
- 2 tsp. dried basil
- 1 bay leaf

1. In a nonstick skillet, cook beef and onion over medium heat until meat is no longer pink, breaking meat into crumbles; drain. Stir in salt and pepper.
2. Transfer to a 5-qt. slow cooker. Add the remaining ingredients. Cover and cook on low for 9-11 hours or until vegetables are tender. Discard bay leaf before serving.
1⅓ cups: 217 cal., 6g fat (2g sat. fat), 40mg chol., 536mg sod., 27g carb. (11g sugars, 3g fiber), 15g pro. **Diabetic exchanges:** 2 lean meat, 2 vegetable, 1 starch.

BEEF VEGETABLE SOUP

THE ULTIMATE CHICKEN NOODLE SOUP

The Ultimate Chicken Noodle Soup

My first winter in Wisconsin was so cold, all I wanted to do was eat hot soup. This version of chicken noodle truly is the ultimate and is a perfect choice for any time of year.
—*Gina Nistico, Denver, CO*

- -

Prep: 15 min. • **Cook:** 45 min. + standing
Makes: 10 servings

2½ lbs. bone-in chicken thighs
½ tsp. salt
½ tsp. pepper
1 Tbsp. canola oil
1 large onion, chopped
1 garlic clove, minced
10 cups chicken broth
4 celery ribs, chopped
4 medium carrots, chopped
2 bay leaves
1 tsp. minced fresh thyme or ¼ tsp. dried thyme
3 cups uncooked kluski or other egg noodles (about 8 oz.)
1 Tbsp. chopped fresh parsley
1 Tbsp. lemon juice
Optional: Additional salt and pepper

1. Pat the chicken thighs dry with paper towels; sprinkle with ½ tsp. pepper and salt. In a 6-qt. stockpot, heat the oil over medium-high heat. Add chicken in batches, skin side down; cook until dark golden brown, 3-4 minutes. Remove chicken from the pan; remove and discard skin. Discard drippings, reserving 2 Tbsp.
2. Add onion to drippings; cook and stir over medium-high heat until tender, 4-5 minutes. Add garlic; cook 1 minute longer. Add broth, stirring to loosen browned bits from pan. Bring to a boil. Return the chicken to pan. Add celery, carrots, bay leaves and thyme. Reduce heat; simmer, covered, until chicken is tender, 25-30 minutes.
3. Transfer chicken to a plate. Remove soup from heat. Add noodles; let stand, covered, until noodles are tender, 20-22 minutes.
4. Meanwhile, when chicken is cool enough to handle, remove meat from bones; discard bones. Shred meat into bite-sized pieces. Return to stockpot. Stir in parsley and lemon juice. Adjust seasoning with additional salt and pepper if desired. Discard bay leaves.
1⅓ cups: 239 cal., 12g fat (3g sat. fat), 68mg chol., 1176mg sod., 14g carb. (3g sugars, 2g fiber), 18g pro.

Contest-Winning New England Clam Chowder

Here in the Pacific Northwest, we dig our own razor clams, and I grind them to make chowder. The canned variety work well, too!
—*Sandy Larson, Port Angeles, WA*

- -

Prep: 20 min. • **Cook:** 35 min.
Makes: 5 servings

4 center-cut bacon strips
2 celery ribs, chopped
1 large onion, chopped
1 garlic clove, minced
3 small potatoes, peeled and cubed
1 cup water
1 bottle (8 oz.) clam juice
3 tsp. reduced-sodium chicken bouillon granules
¼ tsp. white pepper
¼ tsp. dried thyme
⅓ cup all-purpose flour
2 cups fat-free half-and-half, divided
2 cans (6½ oz. each) chopped clams, undrained

1. In a Dutch oven, cook bacon over medium heat until crisp. Remove to paper towels to drain; set aside. Saute celery and onion in the drippings until tender. Add the garlic; cook 1 minute longer. Stir in the potatoes, water, clam juice, chicken bouillon, pepper and thyme. Bring to a boil. Reduce heat; simmer, uncovered, for 15-20 minutes or until potatoes are tender.
2. In a small bowl, combine flour and 1 cup half-and-half until smooth. Gradually stir into the soup. Bring to a boil; cook and stir for 1-2 minutes or until thickened.
3. Stir in the chopped clams and remaining half-and-half; heat through (do not boil). Crumble the cooked bacon; sprinkle over each serving.
1⅓ cups: 260 cal., 4g fat (1g sat. fat), 22mg chol., 788mg sod., 39g carb. (9g sugars, 3g fiber), 13g pro.

TIP

White pepper comes from fully ripened peppercorns that have had their skins removed. It has a milder flavor than black pepper and is great in dishes like mashed potatoes where you might not want black flecks to show. You can always substitute black pepper (perhaps using a bit less than called for) if that's what you have on hand.

CHICKPEA TORTILLA
SOUP, P. 26

Beans & Lentils

Ladle up your favorite legumes to make every bowlful more filling, nutritious and delicious.

ARBORIO RICE
& WHITE BEAN
SOUP, P. 23

EASY PORTUGUESE-STYLE
BEAN SOUP

Easy Portuguese-Style Bean Soup

One day when I was looking at Portuguese recipes, I decided to try making my own that would showcase the bright, spicy flavors of Portugal. My family liked my creation so much, it became one of our staples. The sausage, veggies and herbs can all be prepped in minutes with a food processor.
—*Steven Vance, Woodland, WA*

Prep: 30 min. • **Cook:** 7 hours
Makes: 17 servings

- 4 cans (15½ oz. each) navy beans, rinsed and drained
- 5 cups chicken stock
- 1 lb. linguica sausage or smoked sausage, thinly sliced
- 2 cans (14½ oz. each) petite diced tomatoes, undrained
- 1 large onion, halved and thinly sliced
- 1 large sweet red pepper, thinly sliced
- 2 celery ribs, thinly sliced
- 2 medium carrots, thinly sliced
- 1 cup dry white wine or additional chicken stock
- 4 garlic cloves, minced
- 2 bay leaves
- 1 orange zest strip (3 in.)
- 1 lemon zest strip (3 in.)
- 1 Tbsp. sweet paprika
- 1 Tbsp. hot pepper sauce
- 1 tsp. dried savory
- 1 tsp. dried thyme
- ½ tsp. ground cumin
- ½ tsp. salt
- ¼ tsp. pepper
- ½ cup chopped green onions
- ½ cup minced fresh cilantro
- ½ cup minced fresh parsley

1. Place the first 20 ingredients in a 7-qt. slow cooker. Cook, covered, on low for 7-9 hours or until vegetables are tender. Remove bay leaves and orange and lemon zest strips.
2. Transfer 4 cups soup to a blender; cool slightly. Cover; process until smooth. Return to slow cooker; add green onions, cilantro and parsley. Heat through.
Freeze option: Freeze the cooled soup in freezer containers. To use, partially thaw soup in refrigerator overnight. Heat through in a saucepan, stirring occasionally and adding a little broth if necessary.
1 cup: 235 cal., 8g fat (3g sat. fat), 18mg chol., 893mg sod., 28g carb. (4g sugars, 7g fiber), 14g pro.

FRENCH LENTIL & CARROT SOUP

French Lentil & Carrot Soup

It's amazing how some ingredients can make such a difference in cooking. This soup is no exception! It makes the most of convenient rotisserie chicken, which I can cube in the morning so it's ready to toss in the slow cooker on busy weeknights.
—*Colleen Delawder, Herndon, VA*

Prep: 15 min. • **Cook:** 6¼ hours
Makes: 6 servings

- 5 large carrots, peeled and sliced
- 1½ cups dried green lentils, rinsed
- 1 shallot, finely chopped
- 2 tsp. herbes de Provence
- ½ tsp. pepper
- ¼ tsp. kosher salt
- 6 cups reduced-sodium chicken broth
- 2 cups cubed rotisserie chicken
- ¼ cup heavy whipping cream

1. Combine the first 7 ingredients in a 5- or 6-qt. slow cooker; cover. Cook on low for 6-8 hours or until lentils are tender.
2. Stir in chicken and whipping cream. Cover and continue cooking until heated through, about 15 minutes.
1½ cups: 338 cal., 8g fat (3g sat. fat), 53mg chol., 738mg sod., 39g carb. (5g sugars, 7g fiber), 29g pro. **Diabetic exchanges:** 3 lean meat, 2 starch, 1 vegetable.

TIP

Take a look at the label when purchasing herbes de Provence; some versions of this mixture contain lavender and some do not. The lavender adds a distinctive flavor that complements both lentils and carrots.

Greens & Beans Turkey Soup

On chilly days, we like nothing better than sitting down to a piping hot bowl of soup. This one makes good use of a leftover turkey carcass to create a flavorful stock.
—*Susan Albert, Jonesburg, MO*

Prep: 15 min. • **Cook:** 2½ hours
Makes: 10 servings

- 1 leftover turkey carcass (from a 12-lb. turkey)
- 9 cups water
- 2 celery ribs, cut into ½-in. pieces
- 1 medium onion, cut into chunks
- 1 can (15½ oz.) great northern beans, rinsed and drained
- 1 pkg. (10 oz.) frozen chopped spinach, thawed and squeezed dry
- 3 Tbsp. chopped onion
- 2 tsp. chicken bouillon granules
- 1 tsp. salt
- ¼ tsp. pepper

1. Place turkey carcass in a stockpot; add water, celery and onion. Slowly bring to a boil. Reduce heat; simmer, covered, 2 hours.
2. Remove the carcass and cool. Strain the broth through a cheesecloth-lined colander; discard the vegetables. Skim fat. Remove the meat from the bones and cut into bite-sized pieces; discard bones. Return the broth and meat to pot.
3. Add the beans, spinach, chopped onion, bouillon, salt and pepper. Bring to a boil. Reduce heat; simmer, covered, 10 minutes.
1 cup: 105 cal., 2g fat (0 sat. fat), 22mg chol., 568mg sod., 10g carb. (1g sugars, 3g fiber), 10g pro. **Diabetic exchanges:** 1 lean meat, ½ starch.

Fiesta Chorizo-Chicken Soup

Go south of the border with a slightly spicy specialty chock-full of vegetables, sausage, chicken and more. Add cheesy quesadilla wedges or crusty rolls on the side to round out a hearty, satisfying dinner.
—*Kathy Rodenbeck, Fort Wayne, IN*

Prep: 30 min. • **Cook:** 35 min.
Makes: 12 servings

- 1 lb. uncooked chorizo, casings removed, or bulk spicy pork sausage
- 2 cups sliced fresh carrots
- 1 medium onion, chopped
- 4 garlic cloves, minced
- 1 lb. boneless skinless chicken breasts, cubed
- 1 tsp. salt
- ¼ tsp. pepper
- 2 Tbsp. olive oil
- 3 medium sweet potatoes, peeled and cubed
- 1 pkg. (10 oz.) frozen corn
- 1 medium sweet red pepper, chopped
- 1 carton (32 oz.) reduced-sodium chicken broth
- 1 can (16 oz.) butter beans, rinsed and drained
- 1 can (15 oz.) black beans, rinsed and drained
- 1 can (14½ oz.) fire-roasted diced tomatoes, undrained
- 1 can (5½ oz.) reduced-sodium V8 juice
- 1 tsp. hot pepper sauce
- 2 cups fresh spinach, chopped

1. Crumble the chorizo into a Dutch oven. Add the carrots, onion and garlic. Cook over medium heat until chorizo is fully cooked. Drain; remove and set aside.
2. In the same pan, saute the chicken, salt and pepper in oil until no longer pink. Add sweet potatoes, corn and red pepper; cook 5 minutes longer.
3. Stir in the chorizo mixture, broth, beans, tomatoes, V8 juice and pepper sauce. Bring to a boil. Reduce heat; simmer, uncovered, for 15 minutes or until vegetables are tender. Stir in spinach; cook until wilted.
1½ cups: 336 cal., 15g fat (5g sat. fat), 54mg chol., 1190mg sod., 29g carb. (8g sugars, 6g fiber), 22g pro.

FIESTA CHORIZO-CHICKEN SOUP

ARBORIO RICE &
WHITE BEAN SOUP

Italian Meatball & Bean Soup

Here's a taste of Italy the whole family will enjoy. Zesty from-scratch meatballs make for a complete meal in a bowl.
—*Amanda Bowyer, Caldwell, ID*

Prep: 30 min. • **Cook:** 5 hours
Makes: 6 servings

- 1 large egg
- 3 Tbsp. 2% milk
- ⅓ cup seasoned bread crumbs
- 1 lb. bulk Italian sausage
- ½ lb. ground turkey
- 2 cans (14½ oz. each) diced tomatoes
- 1 can (15 oz.) cannellini beans, rinsed and drained
- 1 can (15 oz.) black beans, rinsed and drained
- 1 can (8 oz.) tomato sauce
- 1 cup water
- 2 green onions, thinly sliced
- 1 tsp. Italian seasoning
- 1 tsp. dried minced garlic
- ½ tsp. crushed red pepper flakes
  Additional thinly sliced green onions, optional

1. In a large bowl, combine the egg, milk and bread crumbs. Crumble sausage and turkey over mixture and mix well. Shape into 1-in. balls. In a large skillet, brown meatballs in batches; drain.

2. Transfer meatballs to a 3-qt. slow cooker. Stir in remaining ingredients. Cover; cook on low 5-6 hours or until thermometer inserted in a meatball reaches 160°. If desired, top servings with additional sliced green onion.

1½ cups: 529 cal., 31g fat (11g sat. fat), 119mg chol., 1273mg sod., 35g carb. (6g sugars, 8g fiber), 27g pro.

Arborio Rice & White Bean Soup

Homemade soup is the ultimate comfort food. This recipe is ready to eat in just 30 minutes, low in fat and absolutely delicious. What's not to love?
—*Deanna McDonald, Muskegon, MI*

Takes: 30 min. • **Makes:** 4 servings

- 1 Tbsp. olive oil
- 3 garlic cloves, minced
- ¾ cup uncooked arborio rice
- 1 carton (32 oz.) vegetable broth
- ¾ tsp. dried basil
- ½ tsp. dried thyme
- ¼ tsp. dried oregano
- 1 pkg. (16 oz.) frozen broccoli-cauliflower blend
- 1 can (15 oz.) cannellini beans, rinsed and drained
- 2 cups fresh baby spinach
  Lemon wedges, optional

1. In a large saucepan, heat oil over medium heat; saute the garlic 1 minute. Add the rice; cook and stir 2 minutes. Stir in the vegetable broth and herbs; bring to a boil. Reduce heat; simmer, covered, until rice is al dente, about 10 minutes.

2. Stir in frozen vegetables and beans; cook, covered, over medium heat until heated through and rice is tender, 8-10 minutes, stirring occasionally. Stir in spinach until wilted. If desired, serve with lemon wedges.

1¾ cups: 303 cal., 4g fat (1g sat. fat), 0 chol., 861mg sod., 52g carb. (2g sugars, 6g fiber), 9g pro.

 TIP

A combo of fresh and frozen veggies makes this soup easy to prepare. The broccoli and cauliflower pieces are on the larger side, but don't shy away from this if you prefer smaller—they'll cut easily with your spoon.

White Bean & Chicken Enchilada Soup

Here's how I satisfy my daughters' craving for creaminess, my husband's for spice and mine for white beans. Garnishes such as shredded cheese, sour cream and tortilla chips add the perfect finishing touch.
—*Darcy Gonzalez, Palmdale, CA*

Prep: 15 min. • **Cook:** 20 min.
Makes: 8 servings

- 4 cans (15½ oz. each) great northern beans, rinsed and drained
- 3 boneless skinless chicken breasts (6 oz. each), cubed
- ½ medium onion, chopped
- 1 garlic clove, minced
- 2 cups frozen corn, thawed
- 1 can (10¾ oz.) condensed cream of chicken soup, undiluted
- 1 carton (32 oz.) reduced-sodium chicken broth
- 1 Tbsp. ground cumin
- 2 seeded and chopped jalapeno peppers, divided
- 1 tsp. pepper
- 2 green onions, chopped
  Sour cream, shredded cheddar cheese and tortilla chips
  Fresh cilantro leaves, optional

1. In a large stockpot, combine the first 8 ingredients. Add 1 chopped jalapeno and ground pepper. Bring to a boil. Reduce heat; simmer, covered, until the chicken is no longer pink and the soup is heated through, 15-20 minutes.
2. Serve with remaining chopped jalapeno; top with green onions, sour cream, cheddar cheese and tortilla chips. If desired, add cilantro leaves.
1½ cups: 301 cal., 5g fat (1g sat. fat), 41mg chol., 1121mg sod., 37g carb. (1g sugars, 12g fiber), 25g pro.

WHITE BEAN & CHICKEN
ENCHILADA SOUP

THE SOUTH
IN A POT SOUP

The South in a Pot Soup

With black-eyed peas, greens and more, this special soup is like having all my favorite childhood food memories together in one big pot. It's a wonderful way to introduce others to black-eyed peas. See the additional directions for making it in a slow cooker.
—*Stephanie Rabbitt-Schapp, Cincinnati, OH*

Prep: 15 min. • **Cook:** 45 min.
Makes: 8 servings

- 1   Tbsp. canola oil
- 1½   lbs. lean ground beef (90% lean)
- 1   large sweet potato, peeled and diced
- 1   large sweet onion, diced
- 1   medium sweet pepper (any color), diced
- 1   can (15½ oz.) black-eyed peas, rinsed and drained
- 1   Tbsp. ground cumin
- 1   Tbsp. curry powder
- ¾   tsp. salt
- ½   tsp. coarsely ground pepper
- 2   cans (14½ oz. each) reduced-sodium beef broth
- 4   cups chopped collard greens or chopped fresh spinach

1. In a Dutch oven, heat oil over medium heat. Cook and stir ground beef, crumbling meat, until no longer pink, 8-10 minutes. Add the sweet potato, onion and pepper; saute until onion and pepper are slightly softened, 4-5 minutes.
2. Add black-eyed peas, cumin, curry, salt and pepper; stir in broth and bring to a boil. Reduce heat; simmer until the sweet potato is almost tender, 15-18 minutes.
3. Add collard greens; cook until tender, 15-18 minutes. If desired, add more cumin and curry.

1¼ cups: 267 cal., 9g fat (3g sat. fat), 55mg chol., 544mg sod., 23g carb. (8g sugars, 5g fiber), 22g pro. **Diabetic exchanges:** 2 lean meat, 1 starch, 1 vegetable, ½ fat.
For slow cooker: In a 4- to 5-qt. slow cooker, crumble the ground beef; add the next 8 ingredients. Pour in enough broth to reach desired consistency. Cook, covered, on low 6-8 hours. A half-hour before serving, skim off any fat; add greens.

Swiss Chard Bean Soup

This bountiful soup combines nutritious Swiss chard with other garden favorites. The light broth is surprisingly flavorful, and the sprinkling of grated Parmesan adds a little richness.
—Taste of Home *Test Kitchen*

Prep: 25 min. • **Cook:** 30 min.
Makes: 10 servings

- 1 medium carrot, coarsely chopped
- 1 small zucchini, coarsely chopped
- 1 small yellow summer squash, coarsely chopped
- 1 small red onion, chopped
- 2 Tbsp. olive oil
- 2 garlic cloves, minced
- 3 cans (14½ oz. each) reduced-sodium chicken broth
- 4 cups chopped Swiss chard
- 1 can (15½ oz.) great northern beans, rinsed and drained
- 1 can (14½ oz.) diced tomatoes, undrained
- 1 tsp. dried thyme
- ½ tsp. salt
- ½ tsp. dried oregano
- ¼ tsp. pepper
- ¼ cup grated Parmesan cheese

1. In a Dutch oven , saute chopped carrot, zucchini, yellow squash and onion in oil until tender. Add garlic; saute 1 minute longer. Add the chicken broth, Swiss chard, beans, tomatoes, thyme, salt, oregano and pepper.
2. Bring to a boil. Reduce heat; simmer, uncovered, for 15 minutes or until chard is tender. Just before serving, sprinkle with Parmesan cheese.
1 cup: 94 cal., 4g fat (1g sat. fat), 2mg chol., 452mg sod., 12g carb. (3g sugars, 4g fiber), 5g pro.

CHICKPEA TORTILLA SOUP

Chickpea Tortilla Soup

In our house, this vegan recipe checks all the boxes—it's filling, healthy and family-friendly. We like to have fun with the toppings by experimenting with different options and combinations each time.
—*Julie Peterson, Crofton, MD*

Takes: 30 min. • **Makes:** 8 servings

- 1 Tbsp. olive oil
- 1 medium red onion, chopped
- 4 garlic cloves, minced
- 1 to 2 jalapeno peppers, seeded and chopped, optional
- ¼ tsp. pepper
- 8 cups vegetable broth
- 1 cup red quinoa, rinsed
- 2 cans (15 oz. each) no-salt-added chickpeas or garbanzo beans, rinsed and drained
- 1 can (15 oz.) no-salt-added black beans, rinsed and drained
- 3 medium tomatoes, chopped
- 1 cup fresh or frozen corn
- ⅓ cup minced fresh cilantro

Optional ingredients: Crushed tortilla chips, cubed avocado, lime wedges and additional chopped cilantro

Heat oil in a Dutch oven over medium-high heat. Add onion, garlic, jalapeno if desired, and pepper; cook and stir until tender, 3-5 minutes. Add broth and quinoa. Bring to a boil; reduce heat. Simmer, uncovered, until the quinoa is tender, about 10 minutes. Add the chickpeas, beans, tomatoes, corn and cilantro; heat through. If desired, serve with optional ingredients.
1½ cups: 289 cal., 5g fat (0 sat. fat), 0 chol., 702mg sod., 48g carb. (5g sugars, 9g fiber), 13g pro.

TIP

The lime in this recipe is optional, but you'll want to give it a try—that little bit of acid really brightens the flavor of the soup.

Hearty Black Bean Soup

Cumin, chili powder and a dash of hot sauce give a tongue-tingling boost to the veggies I simmer in my slow cooker and serve with rice. Have leftover smoked sausage, browned ground beef or roast? Toss it in for the last half-hour of cooking.
—*Amy Chop, Oak Grove, LA*

- -

Prep: 10 min. • **Cook:** 9 hours
Makes: 8 servings

- 3 medium carrots, halved and thinly sliced
- 2 celery ribs, thinly sliced
- 1 medium onion, chopped
- 4 garlic cloves, minced
- 1 can (30 oz.) black beans, rinsed and drained
- 2 cans (14½ oz. each) reduced-sodium chicken broth or vegetable broth
- 1 can (15 oz.) crushed tomatoes
- 1½ tsp. dried basil
- ½ tsp. dried oregano
- ½ tsp. ground cumin
- ½ tsp. chili powder
- ½ tsp. hot pepper sauce
  Hot cooked rice

In a 3-qt. slow cooker, combine the first 12 ingredients. Cover and cook on low for 9-11 hours or until the vegetables are tender. Serve with rice.

1 cup: 129 cal., 0 fat (0 sat. fat), 0 chol., 627mg sod., 24g carb. (6g sugars, 6g fiber), 8g pro. **Diabetic exchanges:** 1½ starch, 1 lean meat.

Country Sausage Soup

When I don't know what to prepare for dinner, I stir together savory pork sausage, two kinds of beans and diced tomatoes for a delicious, satisfying meal in just 20 minutes. It's one I know I can rely on.
—*Grace Meyer, Galva, KS*

- -

Takes: 20 min. • **Makes:** 4 servings

- ¾ lb. bulk pork sausage
- 1 can (14½ oz.) diced tomatoes, undrained
- 1 can (14½ oz.) chicken broth
- 1 tsp. dried thyme
- ¾ to 1 tsp. dried rosemary, crushed
- ¼ tsp. pepper
- 1 can (15½ oz.) great northern beans, rinsed and drained
- 1 can (15 oz.) garbanzo beans or chickpeas, rinsed and drained

In a large saucepan, cook the sausage over medium heat until no longer pink; drain. Stir in tomatoes, chicken broth, thyme, rosemary and pepper. Bring to a boil. Stir in the beans; heat through.

1½ cups: 387 cal., 18g fat (6g sat. fat), 31mg chol., 1279mg sod., 39g carb. (7g sugars, 11g fiber), 17g pro.

HEARTY
BLACK BEAN
SOUP

CREAM OF
CAULIFLOWER
SOUP, P. 35

Cheesy & Creamy

Mmm! Indulge your craving for a bowl of rich, golden goodness with one of these irresistible recipes.

ONION CHEESE SOUP, P. 33

Bacon Cheeseburger Soup

When I tried a soup that tasted just like my favorite burger—from the beef and cheese to the crispy bacon—I became an instant fan.
—*Geoff Bales, Hemet, CA*

Prep: 20 min. • **Cook:** 4 hours
Makes: 6 servings

1½ lbs. lean ground beef (90% lean)
1 large onion, chopped
⅓ cup all-purpose flour
½ tsp. pepper
2½ cups chicken broth
1 can (12 oz.) evaporated milk
1½ cups shredded cheddar cheese
8 slices American cheese, chopped
1½ cups shredded lettuce
2 medium tomatoes, chopped
6 bacon strips, cooked and crumbled

1. In a large skillet, cook and crumble beef with onion over medium-high heat until no longer pink, 6-8 minutes; drain. Stir in flour and pepper; transfer to a 5-qt. slow cooker.
2. Stir in the broth and milk. Cook, covered, on low until flavors are blended, 4-5 hours. Stir in cheeses until melted. Top servings with remaining ingredients.

1 cup: 557 cal., 32g fat (17g sat. fat), 135mg chol., 1160mg sod., 18g carb. (10g sugars, 1g fiber), 42g pro.

 TIP

Turn Bacon Cheeseburger Soup into southwestern fare by flavoring the beef with taco seasonings. Replace some of the cheddar with a Mexican cheese blend, add a few drops of hot sauce and substitute diced avocado for the bacon.

BACON CHEESEBURGER SOUP

CREAMY
RED PEPPER
SOUP

Creamy Red Pepper Soup

Everyone loves this recipe, but no one ever guesses the secret ingredient—pears!
—*Connie Summers, Augusta, MI*

Prep: 15 min. • **Cook:** 30 min. + cooling
Makes: 12 servings

- 2 large onions, chopped
- ¼ cup butter, cubed
- 4 garlic cloves, minced
- 2 large potatoes, peeled and diced
- 2 jars (7 oz. each) roasted red peppers, drained, patted dry and chopped
- 5 cups chicken broth
- 2 cans (15 oz. each) pears in juice
- ⅛ tsp. cayenne pepper
- ⅛ tsp. black pepper
  Optional: Chopped chives, heavy cream and croutons

1. In a Dutch oven, saute onions in butter until tender. Add garlic; cook 1 minute longer. Add the potatoes, red peppers and chicken broth. Bring to a boil. Reduce heat; cover and simmer for 15-20 minutes or until vegetables are tender. Remove from heat. Add pears; let cool.

2. Using a blender, puree soup in batches. Return to the pan. Stir in cayenne pepper and black pepper. Cook until heated through. If desired, serve with chopped chives, heavy cream and croutons.

1 cup: 127 cal., 4g fat (2g sat. fat), 10mg chol., 494mg sod., 20g carb. (9g sugars, 2g fiber), 3g pro.

Cheesy Cream of Asparagus Soup

Kids are often reluctant to eat veggies, but you'll get requests for seconds when you add lots of yummy Monterey Jack cheese .
—*Muriel Lerdal, Humboldt, IA*

Takes: 25 min. • **Makes:** 6 servings

- 2 pkg. (12 oz. each) frozen cut asparagus
- ¼ cup butter
- 2 Tbsp. all-purpose flour
- 4 cups whole milk
- 1 cup shredded Monterey Jack cheese
- 4 to 5 drops hot pepper sauce
- 1½ tsp. salt
- ¾ to 1 tsp. pepper
  Roasted asparagus tips, optional

1. Prepare asparagus according to the package directions; drain and set aside. In a large saucepan, melt the butter. Stir in flour until smooth; gradually add milk. Bring to a boil; cook and stir until thickened, about 2 minutes. Cool slightly.

2. Pour half the milk mixture into a blender; add half the asparagus. Cover and process until very smooth; return soup to the saucepan. Repeat with the remaining milk mixture and asparagus. Stir in cheese, hot pepper sauce, salt and pepper; heat through (do not boil). If desired, top with roasted asparagus tips.

¾ cup: 261 cal., 19g fat (12g sat. fat), 59mg chol., 852mg sod., 12g carb. (9g sugars, 1g fiber), 12g pro.

BROCCOLI BEER CHEESE SOUP

Broccoli Beer Cheese Soup

Whether the beer you choose is nonalcoholic or not, this soup has incredible flavor. I always make extra to freeze in individual servings.
—*Lori Lee, Brooksville, FL*

Prep: 20 min. • **Cook:** 30 min.
Makes: 10 servings

- 3 Tbsp. butter
- 5 celery ribs, finely chopped
- 3 medium carrots, finely chopped
- 1 small onion, finely chopped
- 4 cups fresh broccoli florets, chopped
- ¼ cup chopped sweet red pepper
- 4 cans (14½ oz. each) chicken broth
- ½ tsp. pepper
- ½ cup all-purpose flour
- ½ cup water
- 3 cups shredded cheddar cheese
- 1 pkg. (8 oz.) cream cheese, cubed
- 1 bottle (12 oz.) beer or nonalcoholic beer
  Optional toppings: Additional shredded cheddar cheese, cooked and crumbled bacon strips, chopped green onions, sour cream and salad croutons

1. In a Dutch oven, melt the butter over medium-high heat. Add celery, carrots and onion; saute until crisp-tender. Add broccoli and red pepper; stir in broth and pepper. Combine the flour and water until smooth; gradually stir into pan. Bring to a boil. Reduce heat; simmer, uncovered, until thickened and vegetables are tender, 25-30 minutes.

2. Stir in the cheeses and beer until cheeses are melted (do not boil). Top with additional shredded cheese, bacon, green onions, sour cream and croutons as desired.

Freeze option: Before adding toppings, cool soup; transfer to freezer containers. Freeze up to 3 months. To use, partially thaw in the refrigerator overnight; heat through in a large saucepan over medium-low heat, stirring occasionally (do not boil). Add toppings as desired.

1 cup: 316 cal., 23g fat (13g sat. fat), 69mg chol., 1068mg sod., 13g carb. (5g sugars, 2g fiber), 12g pro.

Creamy Chicken & Broccoli Stew

My husband doesn't care for many chicken dishes, but he requests this stew regularly. Served over mashed potatoes, it satisfies even the heartiest appetites.
—*Mary Watkins, Little Elm, TX*

Prep: 15 min. • **Cook:** 6 hours
Makes: 8 servings

- 8 bone-in chicken thighs, skinned (about 3 lbs.)
- 1 cup Italian salad dressing
- ½ cup white wine or chicken broth
- 6 Tbsp. butter, melted, divided
- 1 Tbsp. dried minced onion
- 1 Tbsp. garlic powder
- 1 Tbsp. Italian seasoning
- ¾ tsp. salt, divided
- ¾ tsp. pepper, divided
- 1 can (10¾ oz.) condensed cream of mushroom soup, undiluted
- 1 pkg. (8 oz.) cream cheese, softened
- 2 cups frozen broccoli florets, thawed
- 2 lbs. red potatoes, quartered

1. Place the chicken in a 4-qt. slow cooker. Combine the Italian salad dressing, wine, 4 Tbsp. butter, onion, garlic powder, Italian seasoning, ½ tsp. salt and ½ tsp. pepper in a small bowl; pour over chicken.
2. Cover and cook on low for 5 hours. Skim fat. Remove the chicken from slow cooker with slotted spoon; shred chicken with 2 forks and return to slow cooker. Combine the cream soup, cream cheese and 2 cups of liquid from slow cooker in a small bowl until blended; add to slow cooker. Cover and cook 45 minutes longer or until chicken is tender, adding the broccoli during the last 30 minutes of cooking.
3. Meanwhile, place potatoes in a large saucepan and cover with water. Bring to a boil. Reduce heat; cover and simmer until tender, 15-20 minutes. Drain and return to pan. Mash potatoes with the remaining butter, salt and pepper.
4. Serve chicken and broccoli mixture with potatoes.

⅔ cup chicken mixture with ½ cup potatoes: 572 cal., 36g fat (14g sat. fat), 142mg chol., 1126mg sod., 28g carb. (5g sugars, 3g fiber), 29g pro.

Onion Cheese Soup

I made a few adjustments to a recipe I came across in a community cookbook. The result was a rich, buttery, cheesy combination that goes together in less than 30 minutes.
—*Janice Pogozelski, Cleveland, OH*

Takes: 25 min. • **Makes:** 6 servings

- 1 large onion, chopped
- 3 Tbsp. butter
- 3 Tbsp. all-purpose flour
- ½ tsp. salt
  Pepper to taste
- 4 cups whole milk
- 2 cups shredded Colby-Monterey Jack cheese
  Seasoned salad croutons
  Optional: Grated Parmesan cheese and minced chives

1. In a large saucepan, saute the onion in butter. Stir in the flour, salt and pepper until blended. Gradually add the milk. Bring to a boil; cook and stir for 2 minutes or until thickened.
2. Stir in the cheese until melted. Serve with croutons and, if desired, top with Parmesan cheese and minced chives.
1 cup: 308 cal., 22g fat (15g sat. fat), 65mg chol., 540mg sod., 14g carb. (9g sugars, 1g fiber), 14g pro.

CREAMY CHICKEN & BROCCOLI STEW

CREAM OF
CAULIFLOWER
SOUP

Cream of Cauliflower Soup

I simmer this mildly cheesy recipe just as often on warm summer days as on cold winter ones. It's so good!
—*Karen Brown, West Lafayette, OH*

- -

Takes: 20 min. • **Makes:** 6 servings

- ⅓ cup thinly sliced green onions (tops only)
- 2 Tbsp. butter
- 2 Tbsp. all-purpose flour
- ½ tsp. salt
- 2 cups chicken broth
- 2¼ cups frozen cauliflower, thawed and chopped
- 2 cups 1% milk
- 1½ cups shredded reduced-fat cheddar cheese
- 2 Tbsp. dry sherry, optional
- 1 Tbsp. minced chives

1. In a saucepan, saute onions in butter until tender. Stir in flour and salt until blended. Gradually add broth. Bring to a boil; cook and stir for 2 minutes or until thickened. Reduce heat.

2. Add cauliflower; simmer for 2 minutes. Add the milk and cheese; cook and stir until cheese is melted. Stir in sherry if desired. Garnish with chives.

1 cup: 186 cal., 11g fat (6g sat. fat), 36mg chol., 792mg sod., 10g carb. (6g sugars, 1g fiber), 13g pro.

SPEEDY CREAM OF WILD RICE SOUP

Speedy Cream of Wild Rice Soup

Want comfort food on the table quickly? Simply dress up canned cream of potato soup with wild rice, Swiss cheese, bacon and a few other ingredients. You'll have a thick, indulgent treat that tastes homemade.
—*Joanne Eickhoff, Pequot Lakes, MN*

- -

Takes: 20 min. • **Makes:** 2 servings

- ½ cup water
- 4½ tsp. dried minced onion
- ⅔ cup condensed cream of potato soup, undiluted
- ½ cup shredded Swiss cheese
- ½ cup cooked wild rice
- ½ cup half-and-half cream
- 2 bacon strips, cooked and crumbled

In a small saucepan, bring water and onion to a boil. Reduce heat. Stir in soup, cheese, wild rice and cream; heat through (do not boil). Garnish with bacon.

1 cup: 333 cal., 18g fat (11g sat. fat), 68mg chol., 835mg sod., 24g carb. (5g sugars, 2g fiber), 15g pro.

Buffalo Chicken Wing Soup

We love Buffalo chicken wings. This has the same zippy flavor. Start with a small amount of hot sauce—you can always add more.
—*Pat Farmer, Falconer, NY*

- -

Prep: 5 min. • **Cook:** 4 hours
Makes: 8 servings

- 5 cups 2% milk
- 3 cans (10¾ oz. each) condensed cream of chicken soup, undiluted
- 3 cups shredded cooked chicken (about 1 lb.)
- 1 cup sour cream
- ¼ to ½ cup Louisiana-style hot sauce
  Optional: Sliced celery and additional hot sauce

In a 5-qt. slow cooker, mix all ingredients. Cook, covered, on low until heated through and flavors are blended, 4-5 hours. If desired, top servings with sliced celery and additional hot sauce.

1⅓ cups: 572 cal., 29g fat (11g sat. fat), 180mg chol., 1308mg sod., 18g carb. (9g sugars, 2g fiber), 57g pro.

Creamy Cremini-Spinach Soup

Cremini mushrooms—often labeled as baby portobellos—make this meatless option a chunky and filling choice. It's perfect with a thick slice of rustic bread.
—*Susan Jordan, Denver, CO*

Prep: 15 min. • **Cook:** 30 min.
Makes: 6 servings

¼ cup butter, cubed
½ lb. sliced baby portobello mushrooms
2 Tbsp. finely chopped celery
2 Tbsp. finely chopped onion
2 Tbsp. all-purpose flour
2½ cups vegetable stock
1 pkg. (6 oz.) fresh baby spinach, chopped
1½ cups half-and-half cream
½ cup sour cream
1½ tsp. salt
¼ tsp. pepper
1 Tbsp. minced fresh parsley

1. In a large saucepan, heat the butter over medium-high heat. Add mushrooms, celery and onion; cook and stir 4-6 minutes or until tender. Stir in flour until blended; cook and stir 2-3 minutes or until lightly browned. Gradually whisk in stock. Bring to a boil. Reduce heat; simmer, covered, 10 minutes.
2. Add spinach; cook and stir 2-4 minutes or until wilted. Gradually stir in the cream, sour cream, salt and pepper; heat through (do not allow to boil). Sprinkle with parsley.
¾ cup: 219 cal., 18g fat (11g sat. fat), 55mg chol., 952mg sod., 8g carb. (4g sugars, 1g fiber), 5g pro.

Swiss Potato Soup

Potatoes, Swiss cheese, onion and bacon? Yes, please! Add just a handful of common pantry staples to the mix and then simmer a pot of pure comfort.
—*Krista Musser, Orrville, OH*

Takes: 30 min. • **Makes:** 4 servings

5 bacon strips, diced
1 medium onion, chopped
2 cups water
4 medium potatoes, peeled and cubed
1½ tsp. salt
⅛ tsp. pepper
⅓ cup all-purpose flour
2 cups 2% milk
1 cup shredded Swiss cheese

1. In a large saucepan, cook the bacon until crisp; remove to paper towels with a slotted spoon. Drain, reserving 1 Tbsp. drippings.
2. Saute the onion in drippings until tender. Add water, potatoes, salt and pepper. Bring to a boil. Reduce heat; simmer, uncovered, for 12 minutes or until potatoes are tender.
3. Combine flour and milk until smooth; gradually stir into the potato mixture. Bring to a boil; cook and stir for 2 minutes or until thickened and bubbly. Remove from the heat; stir in cheese until melted. Sprinkle with bacon.
1 cup: 455 cal., 17g fat (9g sat. fat), 46mg chol., 1218mg sod., 57g carb. (12g sugars, 4g fiber), 21g pro.

SWISS POTATO SOUP

CHICKEN GNOCCHI
PESTO SOUP

Aunt Nancy's Cream of Crab Soup

My sister Nancy is one of the best cooks I know. I put together a cookbook for my daughter of her favorite family recipes— Nancy's soup was a must-have. Our family often had it before church on Christmas Eve.
—Lynne German, Buford, GA

Prep: 10 min. • **Cook:** 25 min.
Makes: 6 servings

- ¼ cup butter, cubed
- 1 tsp. chicken bouillon granules
- 2 Tbsp. finely grated onion
- ¼ cup cornstarch
- 4 cups half-and-half cream
- 1 lb. jumbo lump crabmeat, drained
- 1 Tbsp. grated Parmesan cheese
- 2 tsp. seafood seasoning
- ¼ tsp. salt
- ¼ tsp. ground nutmeg
- ⅛ tsp. pepper
- 3 Tbsp. sherry
  Additional nutmeg

1. In a large saucepan, heat the butter and bouillon over medium heat. Add the onion; cook and stir until tender, 1-2 minutes. Stir in cornstarch until blended; gradually whisk in half-and-half cream. Bring just to a boil, stirring constantly. Stir in the crab, cheese and seasonings. Reduce the heat; simmer, uncovered, to allow flavors to blend, about 20 minutes, stirring occasionally.
2. Stir in the sherry; heat 1-2 minutes longer. Sprinkle servings with additional nutmeg.
¾ cup: 383 cal., 25g fat (16g sat. fat), 175mg chol., 1089mg sod., 12g carb. (6g sugars, 0 fiber), 19g pro.

Chicken Gnocchi Pesto Soup

After tasting a wonderful gnocchi specialty at a restaurant, I created my own quick and tasty version. I love being able to indulge at home any time the mood strikes.
—Deanna Smith, Des Moines, IA

Takes: 25 min. • **Makes:** 4 servings

- 1 jar (15 oz.) roasted garlic Alfredo sauce
- 2 cups water
- 2 cups rotisserie chicken, roughly chopped
- 1 tsp. Italian seasoning
- ¼ tsp. salt
- ¼ tsp. pepper
- 1 pkg. (16 oz.) potato gnocchi
- 3 cups coarsely chopped fresh spinach
- 4 tsp. prepared pesto

In a large saucepan, combine the first 6 ingredients; bring to a gentle boil, stirring occasionally. Stir in gnocchi and spinach; cook until the gnocchi float, 3-8 minutes. Top each serving with pesto.
1½ cups: 586 cal., 26g fat (11g sat. fat), 158mg chol., 1650mg sod., 56g carb. (3g sugars, 4g fiber), 31g pro.

Squash Hominy Soup

Using frozen cooked winter squash speeds up the prep work for this heartwarming recipe. It takes only 20 minutes!
—Taste of Home Test Kitchen

Takes: 20 min. • **Makes:** 4 servings

- ⅔ cup chopped onion
- 1 tsp. minced garlic
- 1 Tbsp. butter
- 2 pkg. (10 oz. each) frozen cooked winter squash, thawed
- 2 cups chicken broth
- 1 can (15½ oz.) hominy, rinsed and drained
- 1 tsp. salt
- ¼ tsp. pepper
- ¼ tsp. each ground ginger, cinnamon and nutmeg
- ¼ cup heavy whipping cream

In a large saucepan, saute onion and garlic in butter until tender. Stir in the squash, broth, hominy and seasonings. Bring to a boil. Reduce heat; cover and simmer for 15 minutes. Remove from heat; stir in cream.
1¼ cups: 203 cal., 9g fat (5g sat. fat), 28mg chol., 1558mg sod., 29g carb. (8g sugars, 7g fiber), 4g pro.

SLOW-COOKER
QUINOA CHILI, P. 47

Chilis

Welcome to the chili cook-off! Beefy, cheesy, vegetarian and spicy—they're all here for you to try.

THAI-STYLE
CHICKEN CHILI, P. 41

HEARTY
VEGETARIAN
CHILI

Hearty Vegetarian Chili

Here's a meatless choice that stands out from the rest. Packed with beans, sun-dried tomatoes, baby portobello mushrooms and vegetarian meat crumbles, it's filling and flavorful enough to fool beef lovers.
—*Pam Ivbuls, Elkhorn, NE*

Takes: 30 min. • **Makes:** 9 servings

- 1¾ cups chopped baby portobello mushrooms
- 1 medium onion, finely chopped
- ½ cup chopped sun-dried tomatoes (not packed in oil)
- 2 Tbsp. olive oil
- 2 garlic cloves, minced
- 1 pkg. (12 oz.) frozen vegetarian meat crumbles
- 2 cans (16 oz. each) chili beans, undrained
- 2 cans (14½ oz. each) no-salt-added diced tomatoes
- ½ cup water
- ½ cup vegetable broth
- 4½ tsp. chili powder
- 2 tsp. brown sugar
- ½ tsp. celery salt
- ½ tsp. ground cumin
- 1 medium ripe avocado, peeled and finely chopped
  Reduced-fat sour cream, optional

1. In a Dutch oven, saute the mushrooms, onion and sun-dried tomatoes in oil until tender. Add the garlic; cook 1 minute longer. Add meat crumbles; heat through.
2. Stir in chili beans, tomatoes, water, broth, chili powder, brown sugar, celery salt and cumin. Bring to a boil. Reduce heat; simmer, uncovered, for 10 minutes. Ladle chili into bowls. Top each with avocado and, if desired, sour cream.
1 cup: 238 cal., 8g fat (1g sat. fat), 0 chol., 611mg sod., 34g carb. (9g sugars, 12g fiber), 14g pro. **Diabetic exchanges:** 2 lean meat, 2 vegetable, 1½ starch, 1 fat.

THAI-STYLE
CHICKEN CHILI

Thai-Style Chicken Chili

Does your family love Thai food? If so, this twist on traditional chicken chili is for you!
—*Roxanne Chan, Albany, CA*

Takes: 30 min. • **Makes:** 6 servings

- 2 Tbsp. sesame oil
- 1 lb. boneless skinless chicken thighs, cut into 1-in. pieces
- 1 medium carrot, diced
- 1 celery rib, chopped
- 1 tsp. minced fresh gingerroot
- 1 large garlic clove, minced
- 1 can (28 oz.) diced tomatoes
- 1 can (13.66 oz.) light coconut milk
- 1 Tbsp. red curry paste
- ¾ tsp. salt
- ¼ tsp. pepper
- 1 cup frozen shelled edamame, thawed
- 2 cups fresh baby spinach
- 1 green onion, minced
- ½ tsp. grated lemon zest
  Fresh cilantro leaves
  Dry roasted peanuts

1. In a large saucepan, heat the sesame oil over medium heat. Add chicken, carrot and celery; cook and stir until vegetables are slightly softened, 3-4 minutes. Add ginger and garlic; cook 1 minute more.
2. Stir in the diced tomatoes, coconut milk, curry paste, salt and pepper. Bring to a boil. Reduce heat; simmer, covered, 10 minutes. Add edamame; cook 5 minutes more. Stir in spinach, green onion and lemon zest until spinach wilts. Remove from heat; top with cilantro and peanuts.
1⅓ cups: 270 cal., 16g fat (6g sat. fat), 50mg chol., 635mg sod., 12g carb. (7g sugars, 4g fiber), 18g pro.

 TIP

Do you enjoy garnishing your chili with sour cream but want a lighter option? Try substituting a dollop of plain Greek yogurt.

Turkey White Chili

Growing up in a Pennsylvania Dutch area, I was surrounded by wonderful cooks and excellent food. Now I enjoy experimenting with new dishes, such as this lighter favorite.
—*Kaye Whiteman, Charleston, WV*

Prep: 15 min. • **Cook:** 70 min.
Makes: 6 servings

- 2 Tbsp. canola oil
- ½ cup chopped onion
- 3 garlic cloves, minced
- 2½ tsp. ground cumin
- 1 lb. boneless skinless turkey breast, cut into 1-in. cubes
- ½ lb. ground turkey
- 3 cups chicken broth
- 1 can (15 oz.) garbanzo beans or chickpeas, rinsed and drained
- 1 Tbsp. minced jalapeno pepper
- ½ tsp. dried marjoram
- ¼ tsp. dried savory
- 2 tsp. cornstarch
- 1 Tbsp. water
  Optional: Shredded Monterey Jack cheese and sliced red onion

1. In a large saucepan or Dutch oven, heat the oil over medium heat. Add onion; saute until tender, about 5 minutes. Add garlic, and cook 1 minute more. Stir in cumin; cook 5 minutes. Add cubed and ground turkey; cook until no longer pink. Add broth, beans, jalapeno, marjoram and savory. Bring to a boil. Reduce the heat; simmer, covered, for 45 minutes, stirring occasionally.
2. Uncover; cook 15 minutes more. Dissolve the cornstarch in water; stir into chili. Bring to a boil. Cook and stir 2 minutes. If desired, serve with cheese and sliced red onion.
1 cup: 288 cal., 12g fat (2g sat. fat), 73mg chol., 635mg sod., 15g carb. (3g sugars, 3g fiber), 29g pro. **Diabetic exchanges:** 3 lean meat, 1 starch, 1 fat.

BLACK BEAN, CHORIZO & SWEET POTATO CHILI

Black Bean, Chorizo & Sweet Potato Chili

Chili is one of my all-time favorite meals. Tossing in black beans, sweet potatoes and spicy sausage is a fantastic change of pace.
—*Julie Merriman, Seattle, WA*

Prep: 20 min. • **Cook:** 6 hours
Makes: 16 servings

- 1 lb. uncooked chorizo, casings removed, or spicy bulk pork sausage
- 1 large onion, chopped
- 2 poblano peppers, finely chopped
- 2 jalapeno peppers, seeded and finely chopped
- 3 Tbsp. tomato paste
- 3 large sweet potatoes, peeled and cut into ½-in. cubes
- 4 cans (14½ oz. each) fire-roasted diced tomatoes, undrained
- 2 cans (15 oz. each) black beans, rinsed and drained
- 2 cups beef stock
- 2 Tbsp. chili powder
- 1 Tbsp. dried oregano
- 1 Tbsp. ground coriander
- 1 Tbsp. ground cumin
- 1 Tbsp. smoked paprika
- ¼ cup lime juice
  Optional: Chopped jalapenos, chopped red onion and crumbled queso fresco

1. In a large skillet, cook and stir the chorizo, onion, poblanos and jalapenos over medium heat for 8-10 minutes or until the chorizo is cooked. Using a slotted spoon, transfer to a 6-qt. slow cooker.
2. Stir in the tomato paste. Add the sweet potatoes, tomatoes, beans, beef stock and spices; stir to combine. Cover and cook on low for 6-7 hours or until potatoes are tender. Stir in lime juice. If desired, top with chopped jalapenos, chopped red onion and crumbled queso fresco.
1 cup: 263 cal., 9g fat (3g sat. fat), 25mg chol., 823mg sod., 33g carb. (11g sugars, 6g fiber), 12g pro.

Cheesy Chili

Here's a popular choice with my grandkids. It's so thick and creamy, you could even serve it as a dip with tortilla chips at parties.
—*Codie Ray, Tallulah, LA*

Takes: 25 min.
Makes: 12 servings

- 2   lbs. ground beef
- 2   medium onions, chopped
- 2   garlic cloves, minced
- 3   cans (10 oz. each) diced tomatoes and green chiles, undrained
- 1   can (28 oz.) diced tomatoes, undrained
- 2   cans (4 oz. each) chopped green chiles
- ½   tsp. pepper
- 2   lbs. Velveeta, cubed

Optional: Sour cream, sliced jalapeno pepper, chopped tomato and minced fresh cilantro

1. In a large saucepan, cook beef, onions and garlic until meat is no longer pink, breaking meat into crumbles; drain. Stir in the tomatoes, chiles and pepper; bring to a boil.
2. Reduce the heat; simmer, uncovered, for 10-15 minutes. Stir in cheese until melted. Serve immediately. If desired, top with sour cream, jalapenos, tomatoes and cilantro.
Freeze option: Freeze the cooled chili in freezer containers; it may be frozen for up to 3 months. To use, partially thaw chili in the refrigerator overnight. Heat through in a saucepan, stirring occasionally; add a little broth or water if necessary.
1 cup: 396 cal., 25g fat (15g sat. fat), 85mg chol., 1166mg sod., 13g carb. (9g sugars, 2g fiber), 29g pro.

CHEESY CHILI

Smoky Peanut Butter Chili

On a whim, I decided to try taking the beans out of my standard chili recipe and adding both peanut butter and peanuts. Wow, was it amazing! My family loved it.
—*Nancy Heishman, Las Vegas, NV*

Prep: 25 min. • **Cook:** 4 hours
Makes: 12 servings

- 1   Tbsp. peanut oil or canola oil
- 2½   lbs. lean ground beef (90% lean)
- 1   large green pepper, chopped
- 1   large red onion, chopped
- 1   large carrot, peeled and chopped
- 2   garlic cloves, minced
- 2   cans (15 oz. each) tomato sauce
- 2   cans (14½ oz. each) diced tomatoes with basil, oregano and garlic, undrained
- 2   cans (4 oz. each) chopped green chiles
- ½   cup creamy peanut butter
- 1   to 2 Tbsp. ground ancho chili pepper
- 1   tsp. kosher salt
- 1   tsp. smoked paprika
       Optional: Shredded smoked cheddar cheese and chopped peanuts

1. In a large skillet, heat oil over medium-high heat; add the beef and cook in batches 7-10 minutes or until no longer pink, breaking into crumbles. Remove with a slotted spoon; drain. Add green pepper, onion and carrot; cook and stir until slightly browned, about 2 minutes. Add garlic; cook 1 minute longer. Transfer meat, vegetables and drippings to a 5- or 6-qt. slow cooker.
2. Stir in next 7 ingredients until combined. Cook, covered, on low until vegetables are tender, about 4 hours. If desired, sprinkle servings with shredded smoked cheddar cheese and chopped peanuts.
1 cup: 279 cal., 15g fat (4g sat. fat), 59mg chol., 878mg sod., 13g carb. (6g sugars, 4g fiber), 23g pro.

Tex-Mex Chili

Need to satisfy big, hearty appetites?
Look no further than a chili brimming
with beef stew meat, plenty of beans
and tasty spices.
—*Eric Hayes, Antioch, CA*

Prep: 20 min. • **Cook:** 6 hours
Makes: 12 servings

- 3 lbs. beef stew meat
- 1 Tbsp. canola oil
- 3 garlic cloves, minced
- 3 cans (16 oz. each) kidney beans, rinsed and drained
- 3 cans (15 oz. each) tomato sauce
- 1 can (14½ oz.) diced tomatoes, undrained
- 1 cup water
- 1 can (6 oz.) tomato paste
- ¾ cup salsa verde
- 1 envelope chili seasoning
- 2 tsp. dried minced onion
- 1 tsp. chili powder
- ½ tsp. crushed red pepper flakes
- ½ tsp. ground cumin
- ½ tsp. cayenne pepper
  Optional: Shredded cheddar cheese, minced fresh cilantro, sour cream, sliced jalapeno or fresno peppers, and additional salsa verde

1. In a large skillet, brown beef in oil in
batches. Add garlic; cook 1 minute longer.
Transfer to a 6-qt. slow cooker.
2. Stir in beans, tomato sauce, tomatoes,
water, tomato paste, salsa verde and
seasonings. Cover and cook on low for
6-8 hours or until meat is tender. Garnish
each serving with toppings as desired.
Freeze option: Before adding toppings, cool
chili. Freeze chili in freezer containers. To use,
partially thaw in refrigerator overnight. Heat
through in a saucepan, stirring occasionally
and adding a little broth or water if necessary.
Garnish with toppings as desired.
1⅓ cups: 334 cal., 9g fat (3g sat. fat), 70mg
chol., 1030mg sod., 31g carb. (7g sugars, 8g
fiber), 32g pro. **Diabetic exchanges:** 3 lean
meat, 1 starch, 1 vegetable.

TEX-MEX CHILI

LIME NAVY BEAN CHILI

Lime Navy Bean Chili

I love being able to make meals like this one using my slow cooker. I simply fill it before leaving in the morning and come home later to a hot, comforting dinner.
—*Connie Thomas, Jensen, UT*

Prep: 15 min. + soaking • **Cook:** 5 hours
Makes: 6 servings

- 1¼ cups dried navy beans
- 3 cups water
- 2 bone-in chicken breast halves (7 oz. each), skin removed
- 1 cup frozen corn
- 1 medium onion, chopped
- 1 can (4 oz.) chopped green chiles
- 4 garlic cloves, minced
- 1 Tbsp. chicken bouillon granules
- 1 tsp. ground cumin
- ½ tsp. chili powder
- 2 Tbsp. lime juice
  Minced fresh cilantro, optional

1. Sort navy beans and rinse with cold water. Place beans in a large saucepan; add water to cover by 2 in. Bring to a boil; boil for 2 minutes. Remove from the heat; cover and let soak until the beans are softened, 1-4 hours. Drain and rinse the beans, discarding liquid.

2. In a 3-qt. slow cooker, combine the beans, water, chicken, corn, onion, chiles, garlic, bouillon, cumin and chili powder. Cover and cook on low until a thermometer reads 170° and beans are tender, 5-6 hours.

3. Remove chicken breasts; set aside until cool enough to handle. Remove meat from the bones; discard bones. Cut chicken into bite-sized pieces; return to slow cooker. Stir in lime juice just before serving. If desired, serve with fresh cilantro.

1 cup: 250 cal., 2g fat (1g sat. fat), 30mg chol., 532mg sod., 37g carb. (5g sugars, 12g fiber), 22g pro. **Diabetic exchanges:** 3 lean meat, 2 starch, 1 vegetable.

Cincinnati Chili

Savor chili the Cincinnati way—spiced with cinnamon, accented with a hint of chocolate flavor and served over spaghetti.
—*Edith Joyce, Parkman, OH*

Prep: 20 min. • **Cook:** 1¾ hours
Makes: 8 servings

- 1 lb. ground beef
- 1 lb. ground pork
- 4 medium onions, chopped
- 6 garlic cloves, minced
- 2 cans (16 oz. each) kidney beans, rinsed and drained
- 1 can (28 oz.) crushed tomatoes
- ¼ cup white vinegar
- ¼ cup baking cocoa
- 2 Tbsp. chili powder
- 2 Tbsp. Worcestershire sauce
- 4 tsp. ground cinnamon
- 3 tsp. dried oregano
- 2 tsp. ground cumin
- 2 tsp. ground allspice
- 2 tsp. hot pepper sauce
- 3 bay leaves
- 1 tsp. sugar
  Salt and pepper to taste
  Hot cooked spaghetti
  Optional: Shredded cheddar cheese, sour cream, chopped tomatoes and green onions

1. In a Dutch oven, cook beef, pork and onions over medium heat until meat is no longer pink, breaking meat into crumbles. Add garlic; cook 1 minute longer. Drain. Add next 13 ingredients, plus salt and pepper to taste; bring to a boil. Reduce heat; cover and simmer for 1½ hours or until heated through.

2. Discard bay leaves. Serve with spaghetti. Garnish with toppings as desired.

1 cup: 421 cal., 16g fat (6g sat. fat), 75mg chol., 443mg sod., 38g carb. (7g sugars, 11g fiber), 32g pro.

Steak & Beer Chili

With the chuck steak, the bratwurst and the pizza sauce, this delicious recipe goes beyond the usual bowlful. I like to dollop a little sour cream on top. If you prefer, substitute beef broth for the beer.
—*Elizabeth King, Duluth, MN*

Prep: 20 min. • **Cook:** 40 min.
Makes: 10 servings

- 1 boneless beef chuck steak (1 lb.), cubed
- 2 Tbsp. canola oil, divided
- 1 lb. uncooked bratwurst links, sliced
- 1 medium onion, chopped
- 4 garlic cloves, minced
- 3 cans (14½ oz. each) diced tomatoes with mild green chiles, undrained
- 2 cans (16 oz. each) hot chili beans, undrained
- 1 bottle (12 oz.) beer or 1½ cups beef broth
- 1 can (14¾ oz.) cream-style corn
- 1 can (8 oz.) pizza sauce
- ½ tsp. chili powder
- ½ tsp. ground cumin
- ¼ tsp. crushed red pepper flakes
  Sour cream, optional

1. In a Dutch oven, brown steak in 1 Tbsp. oil. Remove and keep warm.

2. Add bratwurst, onion and remaining oil to the pan; cook and stir over medium heat until sausage is no longer pink. Add garlic; cook 1 minute longer.

3. Return steak to the pan. Stir in tomatoes, beans, beer, corn, pizza sauce, chili powder, cumin and pepper flakes.

4. Bring to a boil. Reduce the heat; simmer, uncovered, for 25-30 minutes or until heated through. Serve with sour cream if desired.

1⅓ cups: 431 cal., 21g fat (7g sat. fat), 63mg chol., 1317mg sod., 39g carb. (12g sugars, 8g fiber), 23g pro.

STEAK & BEER CHILI

SLOW-COOKER QUINOA CHILI

Lamb & White Bean Chili

After experimenting a bit with lamb and Moroccan seasoning, I ended up creating a new family favorite. I made a second batch almost right away! If you like spicier food, add some harissa paste or use medium salsa instead of mild.
—*Arlene Erlbach, Morton Grove, IL*

Prep: 25 min. • **Cook:** 6¼ hours
Makes: 4 servings

- 1 lb. ground lamb
- 1 cup coarsely chopped red onion
- 1 can (15 oz.) cannellini beans, undrained
- 1 jar (16 oz.) mild chunky salsa
- 3 Tbsp. Moroccan seasoning (ras el hanout), divided
- 4½ tsp. finely chopped lemon zest, divided
- 3 Tbsp. orange marmalade
- ¼ cup minced fresh parsley
- ¼ cup crumbled goat cheese
- 2 Tbsp. sliced almonds
  Optional: Additional chopped red onion and toasted naan flatbread or pita bread

1. In a large nonstick skillet, cook ground lamb and red onion over medium-high heat 6-8 minutes or until no longer pink, breaking into crumbles; drain. Transfer lamb mixture to a 3- or 4-qt. slow cooker. Add beans.
2. In a small bowl, combine salsa, 1½ Tbsp. Moroccan seasoning and 1 Tbsp. lemon zest. Pour over the beans and lamb; stir until well combined. Cook, covered, on low until the onions are tender, about 6 hours.
3. In a small bowl, combine marmalade with remaining Moroccan seasoning and lemon zest; stir into slow cooker. Cook, covered, 15 minutes longer. Sprinkle each serving with parsley, cheese and almonds. If desired, serve with additional red onion and naan or pita bread.
1 cup: 438 cal., 18g fat (8g sat. fat), 84mg chol., 840mg sod., 39g carb. (16g sugars, 7g fiber), 28g pro.

Slow-Cooker Quinoa Chili

This is the dish that turned my husband into a quinoa lover! I made it the day he received good news about a prospective job, and we'll always remember how excited we were as we enjoyed this delightful meal.
—*Claire Gallam, Alexandria, VA*

Prep: 25 min. • **Cook:** 4 hours
Makes: 10 servings

- 1 lb. lean ground beef (90% lean)
- 1 medium onion, chopped
- 2 garlic cloves, minced
- 1 can (28 oz.) diced tomatoes with mild green chiles, undrained
- 1 can (14 oz.) fire-roasted diced tomatoes, undrained
- 1 can (15 oz.) garbanzo beans or chickpeas, rinsed and drained
- 1 can (15 oz.) black beans, rinsed and drained
- 2 cups reduced-sodium beef broth
- 1 cup quinoa, rinsed
- 2 tsp. onion soup mix
- 1 to 2 tsp. crushed red pepper flakes
- 1 tsp. garlic powder
- ¼ to ½ tsp. cayenne pepper
- ¼ tsp. salt
  Optional: Shredded cheddar cheese, chopped avocado, chopped red onion, sliced jalapeno, sour cream and cilantro

1. In a large skillet, cook the ground beef, onion and garlic over medium-high heat 6-8 minutes or until no longer pink, breaking into crumbles; drain.
2. Transfer the mixture to a 5- or 6-qt. slow cooker. Add the next 11 ingredients; stir to combine. Cook, covered, on low 4-5 hours or until quinoa is tender.
3. Serve with optional toppings as desired.
1½ cups: 318 cal., 7g fat (2g sat. fat), 37mg chol., 805mg sod., 41g carb. (7g sugars, 8g fiber), 21g pro. **Diabetic exchanges:** 2½ starch, 2 lean meat.

CHICKEN
ENCHILADA
SOUP, P. 57

Cook It Fast or Slow

Use either a pressure cooker or slow cooker for these versatile recipes. The choice is yours!

ENGLISH PUB SPLIT
PEA SOUP, P. 52

Beefy Cabbage Bean Stew

While we were on a small group quilting retreat, a friend of mine prepared this heartwarming stew one night for dinner. I've been passing around the recipe for others to enjoy ever since.
—*Melissa Glancy, La Grange, KY*

- ½ lb. lean ground beef (90% lean)
- 3 cups shredded cabbage or angel hair coleslaw mix
- 1 can (16 oz.) red beans, rinsed and drained
- 1 can (14½ oz.) diced tomatoes, undrained
- 1 can (8 oz.) tomato sauce
- ¾ cup salsa or picante sauce
- 1 medium green pepper, chopped
- 1 small onion, chopped
- 3 garlic cloves, minced
- 1 tsp. ground cumin
- ½ tsp. pepper
  Shredded cheddar cheese and sliced jalapeno peppers, optional

BEEFY CABBAGE
BEAN STEW

Fast
Prep: 30 min. • **Cook:** 5 min. • **Makes:** 6 servings

1. Select saute or browning setting on a 6-qt. electric pressure cooker; adjust for medium heat. Cook the beef until no longer pink, 6-8 minutes, breaking into crumbles; drain. Press cancel. Return beef to pressure cooker.
2. Stir in the remaining ingredients. Lock lid; close pressure-release valve. Adjust to pressure-cook on high for 3 minutes. Quick-release pressure.

Slow
Prep: 20 min. • **Cook:** 6 hours • **Makes:** 6 servings

1. In a large skillet, cook beef over medium heat 4-6 minutes or until no longer pink, breaking into crumbles; drain.
2. Transfer meat to a 4-qt. slow cooker. Stir in remaining ingredients. Cook, covered, on low 6-8 hours or until cabbage is tender. If desired, top with shredded cheddar cheese and sliced jalapeno peppers.

Freeze option: Freeze cooled stew in freezer containers. To use, partially thaw in refrigerator overnight. Heat through in a saucepan, stirring occasionally and adding a little water if necessary.
1 cup: 177 cal., 4g fat (1g sat. fat), 24mg chol., 591mg sod., 23g carb. (5g sugars, 7g fiber), 13g pro.
Diabetic exchanges: 2 lean meat, 1 starch, 1 vegetable.

Potato Soup

I decided to jazz up a basic potato chowder by adding chopped roasted red peppers. The extra flavor gives a deliciously unique twist to an otherwise ordinary soup.
—*Mary Shivers, Ada, OK*

POTATO
SOUP

- 3 lbs. potatoes, peeled and cut into ½-in. cubes (about 8 cups)
- 1 large onion, chopped
- 1 jar (7 oz.) roasted sweet red peppers, drained and chopped
- 1 small celery rib, chopped
- 6 cups chicken broth
- ½ tsp. garlic powder
- ½ tsp. seasoned salt
- ½ tsp. pepper
- ⅛ tsp. rubbed sage
- ⅓ cup all-purpose flour
- 2 cups heavy whipping cream, divided
- 1 cup grated Parmesan cheese, divided
- 8 bacon strips, cooked and crumbled
- 2 Tbsp. minced fresh cilantro

Fast
Prep: 20 min. • **Cook:** 25 min. • **Makes:** 12 servings

1. Place first 9 ingredients in a 6-qt. electric pressure cooker. Lock lid; close pressure-release valve. Adjust pressure to pressure-cook on high for 15 minutes. Quick-release pressure.
2. Select saute setting and adjust for low heat. Mix flour and ½ cup cream until smooth; stir into soup. Stir in ¾ cup Parmesan cheese, bacon, cilantro and remaining cream. Cook and stir until slightly thickened, 6-8 minutes. Serve with remaining cheese.

Slow
Prep: 20 min. • **Cook:** 5½ hours • **Makes:** 12 servings

1. Place first 9 ingredients in a 5- or 6-qt. slow cooker. Cook, covered, on low 5-6 hours or until potatoes are tender.
2. Mix the flour and ½ cup cream until smooth; stir into the soup. Stir in ¾ cup Parmesan cheese, bacon, cilantro and remaining cream. Cook, covered, on low about 30 minutes or until slightly thickened. Serve with remaining cheese.

1 cup: 289 cal., 19g fat (11g sat. fat), 59mg chol., 848mg sod., 23g carb. (4g sugars, 1g fiber), 7g pro.

TIP
Any combination of potatoes will work in this recipe, but russet potatoes hold up best to the heat.

English Pub Split Pea Soup

This family favorite is the same basic recipe my grandmother used years ago. Now with the convenience of today's appliances, I can spend just 15 minutes doing the prep, walk away for a bit, and then it's soup's on! Finish it with more milk if you like your soup a bit thinner.

—*Judy Batson, Tampa, FL*

1 meaty ham bone	1 Tbsp. prepared English mustard
1⅓ cups dried green split peas, rinsed	½ cup 2% milk
2 celery ribs, chopped	¼ cup minced fresh parsley
1 large carrot, chopped	½ tsp. salt
1 sweet onion, chopped	¼ tsp. pepper
4 cups water	¼ tsp. ground nutmeg
1 bottle (12 oz.) light beer	Minced fresh parsley, optional

Fast

Prep: 15 min. • **Cook:** 15 min. + releasing • **Makes:** 8 servings

1. Place the ham bone in a 6-qt. electric pressure cooker. Add the peas, celery, carrot, sweet onion, water, beer and mustard. Lock lid; close pressure-release valve. Adjust to pressure-cook on high for 15 minutes. Let pressure release naturally.
2. Remove the ham bone from the soup. Cool slightly, trim away fat and remove meat from bone; discard fat and bone. Cut meat into bite-sized pieces; return to pressure cooker. Stir in the remaining ingredients. If desired, top with additional minced parsley.

Slow

Prep: 15 min. • **Cook:** 5 hours • **Makes:** 8 servings

1. Place the ham bone in a 4-qt. slow cooker. Add peas, celery, carrot and sweet onion. Combine water, beer and mustard; pour over the vegetables. Cook, covered, on high 5-6 hours or until peas are tender.
2. Remove the ham bone from the soup. Cool slightly, trim away fat and remove meat from bone; discard fat and bone. Cut meat into bite-sized pieces; return to slow cooker. Stir in remaining ingredients. If desired, top with minced parsley.

1 cup: 141 cal., 1g fat (0 sat. fat), 1mg chol., 193mg sod., 25g carb. (6g sugars, 9g fiber), 9g pro. **Diabetic exchanges:** 1½ starch, 1 lean meat.

 TIP

We used Colman's prepared mustard when testing this recipe. If you can't find English mustard, horseradish mustard is always a good substitute.

ENGLISH PUB
SPLIT PEA SOUP

LENTIL STEW

Lentil Stew

This vegetarian stew is perfect when you want a meatless meal. Adding the cream at the end results in a smoother texture.
—*Michelle Collins, Suffolk, VA*

- 2 Tbsp. canola oil
- 2 large onions, thinly sliced, divided
- 8 plum tomatoes, chopped
- 2 Tbsp. minced fresh gingerroot
- 3 garlic cloves, minced
- 2 tsp. ground coriander
- 1½ tsp. ground cumin
- ¼ tsp. cayenne pepper
- 3 cups vegetable broth
- 2 cups dried lentils, rinsed
- 2 cups water
- 1 can (4 oz.) chopped green chiles
- ¾ cup heavy whipping cream
- 2 Tbsp. butter
- 1 tsp. cumin seeds
- 6 cups hot cooked basmati or jasmine rice
  Optional: Sliced green onions or minced fresh cilantro

Fast
Prep: 45 min. • **Cook:** 15 min. + releasing • **Makes:** 8 servings

1. Select saute setting on a 6-qt. electric pressure cooker. Adjust for medium heat; add oil. When oil is hot, cook and stir half the onions until crisp-tender, 2-3 minutes. Add plum tomatoes, ginger, garlic, coriander, cumin and cayenne; cook and stir 1 minute longer. Press cancel. Stir in broth, lentils, water, green chiles and remaining onion.
2. Lock lid; close pressure-release valve. Adjust to pressure-cook on high for 15 minutes. Let pressure release naturally. Just before serving, stir in cream. In a small skillet, heat butter over medium heat. Add the cumin seeds; cook and stir until golden brown, 1-2 minutes. Add to lentil mixture.
3. Serve with rice. If desired, sprinkle with sliced green onions or minced cilantro.

Slow
Prep: 45 min. • **Cook:** 6 hours • **Makes:** 8 servings

1. In a large skillet, saute half the onions in oil until tender. Add ginger and garlic; saute for 1 minute. Add the tomatoes, coriander, cumin and cayenne; cook and stir 5 minutes longer.
2. In a 4- or 5-qt. slow cooker, combine the vegetable broth, lentils, water, green chiles, tomato mixture and remaining onion. Cover and cook on low 6-8 hours or until lentils are tender.
3. In a small skillet, heat butter over medium heat. Add the cumin seeds; cook and stir until golden brown, 1-2 minutes. Add to lentil mixture. Just before serving, stir cream into slow cooker.
4. To serve, spoon over rice. If desired, sprinkle with sliced green onions or minced cilantro.

1⅓ cups stew with ¾ cup rice: 499 cal., 16g fat (7g sat. fat), 38mg chol., 448mg sod., 72g carb. (5g sugars, 17g fiber), 17g pro.

Easy Pork Posole

Looking for a complete dinner in a bowl? Sit down and dig into a rich, hearty Mexican classic brimming with cubed pork, sliced sausage, hominy and more.
—*Greg Fontenot, The Woodlands, TX*

- 1 Tbsp. canola oil
- ½ lb. boneless pork shoulder butt roast, cubed
- ½ lb. fully cooked andouille sausage links, sliced
- 6 cups reduced-sodium chicken broth
- 2 medium tomatoes, seeded and chopped
- 1 can (15 oz.) hominy, rinsed and drained
- 1 cup minced fresh cilantro
- 1 medium onion, chopped
- 4 green onions, chopped
- 1 jalapeno pepper, seeded and chopped
- 2 garlic cloves, minced
- 1 Tbsp. chili powder
- 1 tsp. ground cumin
- ½ tsp. cayenne pepper
- ½ tsp. coarsely ground pepper
  Optional: Corn tortillas, chopped onion, minced fresh cilantro and lime wedges

EASY PORK POSOLE

Fast

Prep: 30 min. • **Cook:** 10 min. + releasing • **Makes:** 8 servings

1. Select saute setting on a 6-qt. electric pressure cooker and adjust for medium heat. Add oil. When oil is hot, cook and stir pork cubes and sausage links until browned; drain. Return meats to the pressure cooker. Press cancel.

2. Add the next 12 ingredients. Lock lid and close pressure-release valve. Adjust to pressure-cook on high for 10 minutes. Let pressure naturally release for 5 minutes, then quick-release any remaining pressure. If desired, serve with corn tortillas, chopped onion, minced cilantro and lime wedges.

Slow

Prep: 30 min. • **Cook:** 6 hours • **Makes:** 8 servings

1. In a large skillet, heat oil over medium-high heat. Brown pork cubes and sausage links; drain. Transfer to a 4-qt. slow cooker.

2. Stir in chicken broth, tomatoes, hominy, cilantro, onion, green onions, jalapeno, garlic, chili powder, cumin, cayenne and pepper. Cook, covered, on low 6-8 hours or until the meat is tender. If desired, serve with corn tortillas, chopped onion, minced cilantro and lime wedges.

Note: Wear disposable gloves when cutting hot peppers; the oils can burn skin. Avoid touching your face.

1 cup: 190 cal., 11g fat (3g sat. fat), 54mg chol., 957mg sod., 12g carb. (2g sugars, 3g fiber), 14g pro.

CHICKEN
ENCHILADA
SOUP

Nutrition Facts

Chicken Enchilada Soup

This soup delivers a big bowl of fresh comfort. For my husband and me, tasty toppings like avocado, sour cream and tortilla strips are a must.
—*Heather Sewell, Harrisonville, MO*

1 Tbsp. canola oil	2 Tbsp. tomato paste
2 Anaheim or poblano peppers, finely chopped	1 Tbsp. chili powder
1 medium onion, chopped	2 tsp. ground cumin
3 garlic cloves, minced	½ tsp. pepper
1 lb. boneless skinless chicken breasts	½ to 1 tsp. chipotle hot pepper sauce, optional
1 carton (48 oz.) chicken broth	⅓ cup minced fresh cilantro
1 can (14½ oz.) Mexican diced tomatoes, undrained	Optional: Shredded cheddar cheese, cubed avocado, sour cream and tortilla strips
1 can (10 oz.) enchilada sauce	

Fast

Prep: 25 min. • **Cook:** 20 min. + releasing • **Makes:** 8 servings

1. Select saute setting on a 6-qt. electric pressure cooker and adjust for high heat; add the oil. Add the peppers and onion; cook and stir 6-8 minutes or until tender. Add garlic; cook 1 minute longer. Add chicken, broth, tomatoes, enchilada sauce, tomato paste, seasonings and, if desired, pepper sauce. Stir. Lock lid; close pressure-release valve. Adjust to pressure-cook on high for 8 minutes. Allow pressure to naturally release for 7 minutes, then quick-release any remaining pressure.
2. Remove chicken from the pressure cooker. Shred with 2 forks; return to pressure cooker. Stir in the cilantro. Serve with toppings as desired.

Slow

Prep: 25 min. • **Cook:** 6 hours • **Makes:** 8 servings

1. In a large skillet, heat the oil over medium heat. Add the peppers and onion; cook and stir until tender, 6-8 minutes. Add the garlic; cook 1 minute longer. Transfer the pepper mixture and chicken to a 5- or 6-qt. slow cooker. Stir in the broth, tomatoes, enchilada sauce, tomato paste, seasonings and, if desired, pepper sauce. Cook, covered, on low 6-8 hours or until chicken is tender (a thermometer should read at least 165°).
2. Remove chicken from slow cooker. Shred with 2 forks; return to slow cooker. Stir in cilantro. Serve with toppings as desired.

Freeze option: Freeze cooled soup in freezer containers. To use, partially thaw in refrigerator overnight. Heat through in a saucepan, stirring occasionally and adding a little water if necessary.
1½ cups: 125 cal., 4g fat (1g sat. fat), 35mg chol., 1102mg sod., 9g carb. (4g sugars, 3g fiber), 14g pro.

 TIP

To make a fresh garlic clove easy to peel, gently crush it with the flat side of a large knife blade to loosen the peel. If you don't have a large knife handy, crush the garlic with a small can. The peel will come right off.

ITALIAN SAUSAGE
& KALE SOUP

Italian Sausage & Kale Soup

When I tried this colorful soup, our home smelled wonderful—and our meal was just as good! We knew the recipe was a keeper to help get us through cold winter days.
—*Sarah Stombaugh, Chicago, IL*

1   lb. bulk hot Italian sausage
6   cups chopped fresh kale
2   cans (15½ oz. each) great northern beans, rinsed and drained
1   can (28 oz.) crushed tomatoes
4   large carrots, finely chopped (about 3 cups)
1   medium onion, chopped
3   garlic cloves, minced
1   tsp. dried oregano
¼   tsp. salt
⅛   tsp. pepper
5   cups chicken stock
    Grated Parmesan cheese

Fast

Prep: 20 min. • **Cook:** 15 min. + releasing • **Makes:** 8 servings

1. Select saute setting on a 6-qt. electric pressure cooker and adjust for medium heat. Add sausage. Cook and stir, crumbling meat until no longer pink. Press cancel. Remove sausage; drain. Return sausage to pressure cooker.
2. Add the next 10 ingredients. Lock lid; close the pressure-release valve. Adjust to pressure-cook on high for 10 minutes. Let pressure naturally release for 5 minutes; quick-release any remaining pressure.
3. Top each serving with cheese.

Slow

Prep: 20 min. • **Cook:** 8 hours • **Makes:** 8 servings

1. In a large skillet, cook sausage over medium heat for 6-8 minutes or until no longer pink, breaking into crumbles; drain. Transfer to a 5-qt. slow cooker.
2. Add kale, beans, tomatoes, carrots, onion, garlic, seasonings and stock to slow cooker. Cook, covered, on low 8-10 hours or until vegetables are tender.
3. Top each serving with cheese.

1¾ cups: 297 cal., 13g fat (4g sat. fat), 31mg chol., 1105mg sod., 31g carb. (7g sugars, 9g fiber), 16g pro.

Manchester Stew

While in college, I studied abroad. I was a vegetarian at the time and pleasantly surprised by how delicious and diverse vegetarian food in Britain could be. After returning to the States, I re-created my favorite restaurant dish and named it after the University of Manchester. Whenever that enticing aroma fills my kitchen, I feel like I'm back in England!
—*Kimberly Hammond, Kingwood, TX*

- 2 Tbsp. olive oil
- 2 medium onions, chopped
- 2 garlic cloves, minced
- 1 tsp. dried oregano
- 1 cup dry red wine
- 1 lb. small red potatoes, quartered
- 1 can (16 oz.) kidney beans, rinsed and drained
- ½ lb. sliced fresh mushrooms
- 2 medium leeks (white portion only), sliced
- 1 cup fresh baby carrots
- 2½ cups water
- 1 can (14½ oz.) no-salt-added diced tomatoes
- 1 tsp. dried thyme
- ½ tsp. salt
- ¼ tsp. pepper
  Fresh basil leaves

MANCHESTER STEW

Fast
Prep: 25 min. • **Cook:** 5 min. + releasing • **Makes:** 6 servings

1. Select saute setting on a 6-qt. electric pressure cooker. Adjust for medium heat; add the oil. When oil is hot, cook and stir the onions until crisp-tender, 2-3 minutes. Add the garlic and oregano; cook and stir 1 minute longer. Stir in the wine. Bring to a boil; cook until liquid is reduced by half, 3-4 minutes. Press cancel.
2. Add potatoes, beans, mushrooms, leeks and carrots. Stir in water, tomatoes, thyme, salt and pepper. Lock lid; close pressure-release valve. Adjust to pressure-cook on high for 3 minutes. Let pressure release naturally for 10 minutes; quick-release any remaining pressure. Top with basil.

Slow
Prep: 25 min. • **Cook:** 8 hours • **Makes:** 6 servings

1. In a large skillet, heat the oil over medium-high heat. Add onions; cook and stir until crisp-tender, 2-3 minutes. Add garlic and oregano; cook and stir 1 minute longer. Stir in wine. Bring to a boil; cook until liquid is reduced by half, 3-4 minutes.
2. Transfer to a 5- or 6-qt. slow cooker. Add the potatoes, beans, mushrooms, leeks and carrots. Stir in the water, tomatoes, thyme, salt and pepper. Cook, covered, on low 8-10 hours or until the potatoes are tender. Top with basil.

1⅔ cups: 221 cal., 5g fat (1g sat. fat), 0 chol., 354mg sod., 38g carb. (8g sugars, 8g fiber), 8g pro.
Diabetic exchanges: 2 starch, 1 vegetable, 1 fat.

FROGMORE
STEW, P. 64

Fish & Seafood

What's the catch of the day? Soups and stews brimming with fresh, flavorful ingredients!

THAI SHRIMP
SOUP, P. 69

Asian Ramen Shrimp Soup

A package of ramen noodles really speeds up assembly of this colorful broth. You'll need just 15 minutes and only a handful of ingredients to put it together.
—*Donna Hellinger, Lorain, OH*

Takes: 15 min. • **Makes:** 4 servings

- 3½ cups water
- 1 pkg. (3 oz.) Oriental ramen noodles
- 1 cup cooked small shrimp, peeled and deveined
- ½ cup chopped green onions
- 1 medium carrot, julienned
- 2 Tbsp. soy sauce

1. In a large saucepan, bring water to a boil. Set aside seasoning packet from noodles. Add the noodles to boiling water; cook and stir for 3 minutes.

2. Add the shrimp, onions, carrot, soy sauce and contents of seasoning packet. Cook until heated through, 3-4 minutes longer.

1 cup: 148 cal., 4g fat (2g sat. fat), 83mg chol., 857mg sod., 17g carb. (2g sugars, 1g fiber), 12g pro. **Diabetic exchanges:** 1 starch, 1 lean meat.

Jazzed-Up Clam Chowder

Canned clam chowder gets a home-style makeover when I add corn, bacon, cheese, milk and chives. No one ever guesses how quick and easy the recipe is.
—*Josephine Piro, Easton, PA*

Takes: 10 min. • **Makes:** 4 servings

- 1 can (19 oz.) chunky New England clam chowder
- 1 can (8¼ oz.) cream-style corn
- ⅔ cup 2% milk
- 2 Tbsp. shredded cheddar cheese
- 2 Tbsp. bacon bits
- 2 Tbsp. minced chives

In a 1½-qt. microwave-safe dish, combine clam chowder, corn and milk. Cover and microwave on high until heated through, 4-6 minutes, stirring every 2 minutes. Sprinkle servings with cheddar cheese, bacon and chives.

1 cup: 211 cal., 10g fat (5g sat. fat), 14mg chol., 780mg sod., 24g carb. (5g sugars, 2g fiber), 8g pro.

Creamy Seafood Bisque

My deceptively simple bisque makes a special first course—or even a complete meal with a salad or bread. I like to top bowlfuls with shredded Parmesan and green onions.
—*Wanda Allende, Orlando, FL*

Prep: 25 min. • **Cook:** 25 min.
Makes: 8 servings

- ½ cup butter, cubed
- 1 medium red onion, chopped
- 1 cup sliced fresh mushrooms
- 2 garlic cloves, minced
- ½ cup all-purpose flour
- 1 tsp. salt
- 1 tsp. coarsely ground pepper
- 2 Tbsp. tomato paste
- 1 carton (32 oz.) chicken broth
- 2 cups whole baby clams, drained
- ½ lb. uncooked medium shrimp, peeled and deveined
- 2 cups lump crabmeat, drained
- 2 cups heavy whipping cream
- ½ cup shredded Parmesan cheese
- 2 green onions, thinly sliced

1. In a Dutch oven, heat the butter over medium-high heat. Add the red onion and mushrooms; saute for 4-5 minutes or until tender. Add garlic; cook 1 minute longer. Stir in flour, salt and pepper until blended; add tomato paste. Gradually whisk in broth; bring to a boil. Reduce heat; cover and simmer for 5 minutes.

2. Add clams and shrimp; return to a boil. Reduce the heat; simmer, uncovered, 5-10 minutes longer or until shrimp turn pink, stirring occasionally. Stir in crab and cream; heat through (do not boil). Serve with cheese and green onions.

1¼ cups: 453 cal., 36g fat (22g sat. fat), 197mg chol., 1232mg sod., 12g carb. (2g sugars, 1g fiber), 20g pro.

CREAMY SEAFOOD BISQUE

HALIBUT & POTATO CHOWDER

Turkey Shrimp Gumbo

Here's a lighter take on a Louisiana classic. Savor the taste while cutting the calories!
—*Michael Williams, Westfield, NY*

Prep: 10 min. • **Cook:** 2 hours 5 min.
Makes: 10 servings

- 1 tsp. salt
- 1 tsp. pepper
- 1 tsp. cayenne pepper
- 2 lbs. uncooked skinless turkey breast, cubed
- ½ cup vegetable oil, divided
- ½ cup all-purpose flour
- 1 large onion, chopped
- 1 cup chopped celery
- 1 cup chopped sweet red pepper
- 4 garlic cloves, minced
- 4 cups chicken broth
- 2 cups sliced okra
- 4 green onions, sliced
- 10 oz. uncooked medium shrimp, peeled and deveined
- 5 cups hot cooked rice

1. In a small bowl, combine the salt and peppers; sprinkle over turkey. In a Dutch oven, brown turkey in 2 Tbsp. oil; remove with a slotted spoon. Add remaining oil and flour, scraping the pan bottom to loosen browned bits. Cook over medium-low heat for 25-30 minutes until dark brown in color, stirring occasionally.
2. Add onion, celery, red pepper and garlic. Cook over medium heat until the vegetables are crisp-tender, 4-5 minutes. Gradually stir in broth. Bring to a boil. Reduce heat; cover and simmer for 30 minutes. Return turkey to pan; cover and simmer for 30-45 minutes or until turkey is tender. Add okra and green onions; simmer 10 minutes. Add shrimp; simmer until shrimp turn pink, 4-5 minutes. Serve over rice.

1 cup with ½ cup rice: 381 cal., 13g fat (2g sat. fat), 88mg chol., 777mg sod., 33g carb. (3g sugars, 2g fiber), 30g pro.

Halibut & Potato Chowder

I have a passion for cooking and entertaining. Several times a year, I host a dinner party for my retired and current teaching friends. When I served this halibut dish as part of the menu, guests couldn't get enough.
—*Teresa Lueck, Onamia, MN*

Prep: 25 min. • **Cook:** 30 min.
Makes: 12 servings

- ½ cup butter, cubed
- 4 celery ribs, chopped
- 3 medium carrots, chopped
- 1 large onion, chopped
- ½ cup all-purpose flour
- ¼ tsp. white pepper
- 2 cups 2% milk
- 1 can (14½ oz.) chicken broth
- ¼ cup water
- 1 Tbsp. chicken base
- 3 medium potatoes, peeled and chopped
- 1 can (15¼ oz.) whole kernel corn, drained
- 3 bay leaves
- 2 cups half-and-half cream
- 2 Tbsp. lemon juice
- 1 lb. halibut or other whitefish fillets, cut into 1-in. pieces
- 1 cup salad croutons
- ¾ cup grated Parmesan cheese
- ½ cup minced chives

1. In a large saucepan, melt the butter over medium heat. Add the celery, carrots and onion; cook and stir until tender. Stir in flour and pepper until blended; gradually add milk, chicken broth, water and chicken base. Bring to a boil; cook and stir until thickened, about 2 minutes.
2. Add potatoes, corn and bay leaves. Return to a boil. Reduce the heat; cover and simmer until potatoes are tender, 15-20 minutes.
3. Stir in the cream and lemon juice; return to a boil. Add halibut. Reduce heat; simmer, uncovered, until fish flakes easily with a fork, 7-11 minutes. Discard bay leaves. Serve with remaining ingredients.

1 cup: 316 cal., 16g fat (9g sat. fat), 61mg chol., 671mg sod., 25g carb. (8g sugars, 2g fiber), 16g pro.

MARYLAND-STYLE
CRAB SOUP

Frogmore Stew

This medley of shrimp, kielbasa and more is a South Carolina specialty. It's commonly referred to as Frogmore stew or Beaufort stew in recognition of the low country communities that lay claim to its origin. No matter what you call it, this one-pot wonder won't disappoint!
—Taste of Home *Test Kitchen*

Prep: 10 min. • **Cook:** 35 min.
Makes: 8 servings

- 16 cups water
- 1 large sweet onion, quartered
- 3 Tbsp. seafood seasoning
- 2 medium lemons, halved, optional
- 1 lb. small red potatoes
- 1 lb. smoked kielbasa or fully cooked hot links, cut into 1-in. pieces
- 4 medium ears sweet corn, cut into thirds
- 2 lbs. uncooked medium shrimp, peeled and deveined
  Seafood cocktail sauce
  Melted butter
  Additional seafood seasoning

1. In a stockpot, combine the water, onion, seafood seasoning and, if desired, lemons; bring to a boil. Add the red potatoes; cook, uncovered, 10 minutes. Add kielbasa and corn; return to a boil. Reduce heat; simmer, uncovered, 10-12 minutes or until potatoes are tender. Add shrimp; cook 2-3 minutes longer or until shrimp turn pink.
2. Drain; transfer to a bowl. Serve stew with seafood cocktail sauce, butter and additional seafood seasoning.

1 serving: 369 cal., 18g fat (6g sat. fat), 175mg chol., 751mg sod., 24g carb. (7g sugars, 2g fiber), 28g pro.

 TIP

The great thing about most stews is that you can toss in nearly anything you'd like. Add some chopped sweet red pepper, mushrooms or even a jalapeno.

Maryland-Style Crab Soup

Stir seafood into homemade veggie soup for a comforting combination you'll want again and again. I prefer using whole crabs and claws that I've broken into pieces.
—Freelove Knott, Palm Bay, FL

Prep: 20 min. • **Cook:** 6¼ hours
Makes: 8 servings

- 2 cans (14½ oz. each) diced tomatoes with green peppers and onions, undrained
- 2 cups water
- 1½ lbs. potatoes, cut into ½-in. cubes (about 5 cups)
- 2 cups cubed peeled rutabaga
- 2 cups chopped cabbage
- 1 medium onion, finely chopped
- 1 medium carrot, sliced
- ½ cup frozen corn, thawed
- ½ cup frozen lima beans, thawed
- ½ cup frozen peas, thawed
- ½ cup cut fresh green beans (1-in. pieces)
- 4 tsp. seafood seasoning
- 1 tsp. celery seed
- 1 vegetable bouillon cube
- ¼ tsp. salt
- ¼ tsp. pepper
- 1 lb. fresh or lump crabmeat, drained

1. In a 6-qt. slow cooker, combine the first 16 ingredients. Cook, covered, on low 6-8 hours or until vegetables are tender.
2. Stir in the crab. Cook, covered, on low 15 minutes longer or until heated through.
1½ cups: 202 cal., 1g fat (0 sat. fat), 55mg chol., 1111mg sod., 34g carb. (11g sugars, 7g fiber), 15g pro.
Note: This recipe was prepared with Knorr vegetable bouillon.

FROGMORE
STEW

Spicy Seafood Stew

The hardest part about putting together this zippy stew is peeling and dicing the potatoes—and you can do that the night before. Just place the spuds in water and store them in the fridge overnight to speed up assembly the next day.
—*Bonnie Marlow, Ottoville, OH*

- -

Prep: 30 min. • **Cook:** 4¾ hours
Makes: 9 servings

- 2 lbs. potatoes, peeled and diced
- 1 lb. carrots, sliced
- 1 jar (24 oz.) pasta sauce
- 2 jars (6 oz. each) sliced mushrooms, drained
- 1½ tsp. ground turmeric
- 1½ tsp. minced garlic
- 1 tsp. cayenne pepper
- ¼ tsp. salt
- 1½ cups water
- 1 lb. sea scallops
- 1 lb. uncooked shrimp (31-40 per lb.), peeled and deveined

In a 5-qt. slow cooker, combine the first 8 ingredients. Cook, covered, on low until potatoes are tender, 4½-5 hours. Stir in water, scallops and shrimp. Cook, covered, until scallops are opaque and shrimp turn pink, 15-20 minutes longer.
1 cup: 229 cal., 2g fat (0 sat. fat), 73mg chol., 803mg sod., 34g carb. (10g sugars, 6g fiber), 19g pro.

COCONUT SHRIMP CHOWDER

Coconut Shrimp Chowder

After sampling an unforgettable coconut specialty at a Thai restaurant, I decided to try pouring a can of coconut milk into my usual chowder. It was perfection!
—*Michalene Baskett, Decatur, GA*

- -

Takes: 30 min. • **Makes:** 5 servings

- 1 medium onion, chopped
- 2 tsp. canola oil
- ¼ tsp. cayenne pepper
- 2 cups chicken broth
- 1 pkg. (10 oz.) frozen corn
- ¼ tsp. salt
- ¼ tsp. pepper
- 1 can (13.66 oz.) coconut milk
- 1 lb. uncooked medium shrimp, peeled and deveined
- ¼ cup lime juice
- 2 Tbsp. minced fresh cilantro
- 1 medium ripe avocado, peeled and cubed

1. In a large saucepan, saute onion in oil until tender. Add cayenne pepper. Stir in broth, corn, salt and pepper. Bring to a boil. Reduce heat; simmer, uncovered, for 5 minutes. Remove from the heat and stir in coconut milk. Cool slightly.

2. In a food processor, process the soup in batches until blended. Return all to pan. Add the shrimp; cook and stir over medium heat for 5-6 minutes or until shrimp turn pink. Stir in lime juice and cilantro. Garnish servings with avocado.
1 cup: 376 cal., 26g fat (16g sat. fat), 112mg chol., 633mg sod., 22g carb. (4g sugars, 5g fiber), 20g pro.

TIP

Toasted coconut makes a wonderful change-of-pace garnish for this chowder, adding both flavor and texture.

Salmon Dill Soup

My husband enjoys salmon so much that he could eat it every single day of the week. Whenever I get that fish, I try to prepare something special as a treat for both of us. He declared this creamy, chunky soup to be the best I've ever made.
—*Hidemi Walsh, Plainfield, IN*

Takes: 30 min. • **Makes:** 2 servings

- 1 large potato, peeled and cut into 1½-in. pieces
- 1 large carrot, cut into ½-in.-thick slices
- 1½ cups water
- 1 cup reduced-sodium chicken broth
- 5 medium fresh mushrooms, halved
- 1 Tbsp. all-purpose flour
- ¼ cup reduced-fat evaporated milk
- ¼ cup shredded part-skim mozzarella cheese
- ½ lb. salmon fillet, cut into 1½-in. pieces
- ¼ tsp. pepper
- ⅛ tsp. salt
- 1 Tbsp. chopped fresh dill

1. Place the first 4 ingredients in a saucepan; bring to a boil. Reduce the heat to medium; cook, uncovered, until vegetables are tender, 10-15 minutes.

2. Add mushrooms. In a small bowl, mix flour and milk until smooth; stir into soup. Return to a boil; cook and stir until mushrooms are tender. Reduce heat to medium; stir in the cheese until melted.

3. Reduce heat to medium-low. Add salmon; cook, uncovered, until the fish just begins to flake easily with a fork, 3-4 minutes. Stir in pepper and salt. Sprinkle with dill.

2½ cups: 398 cal., 14g fat (4g sat. fat), 71mg chol., 647mg sod., 37g carb. (7g sugars, 3g fiber), 30g pro. **Diabetic exchanges:** 3 lean meat, 2½ starch.

Curry Shrimp & Rice

My family and I love curry shrimp and rice. Here's one of my favorite recipes—most of the ingredients come straight out of the pantry. To add heat, just stir in 1 tablespoon of fresh ground chili paste.
—*Angela Spengler, Niceville, FL*

Prep: 10 min. • **Cook:** 25 min.
Makes: 8 servings

- 2 Tbsp. butter
- ½ medium onion, chopped
- 1 carton (32 oz.) chicken broth
- 2 cans (14½ oz. each) diced potatoes, drained
- 2 cans (7 oz. each) white or shoepeg corn, drained
- 1 can (13.66 oz.) coconut milk
- 1 can (8 oz.) bamboo shoots, drained
- 1 Tbsp. curry powder
- 1 to 3 tsp. Thai red chili paste, optional
- ½ tsp. salt
- ½ tsp. pepper
- 12 oz. peeled and deveined cooked shrimp (61-70 per lb.)
- 2 pkg. (8.8 oz. each) ready-to-serve long grain rice
  Optional: Lime wedges and fresh basil

1. In a Dutch oven, heat the butter over medium-high heat. Add onion; cook and stir until tender, 4-5 minutes. Add broth, potatoes, corn, coconut milk, bamboo shoots, curry powder, chili paste if desired, salt and pepper. Bring to a boil; reduce heat. Simmer, uncovered, until the flavors have blended, 12-15 minutes, stirring occasionally.

2. Add shrimp; heat through. Prepare rice according to package directions; serve with curry. Sprinkle with additional curry powder. If desired, serve with lime wedges and basil.

1 serving: 354 cal., 13g fat (10g sat. fat), 75mg chol., 1112mg sod., 42g carb. (3g sugars, 3g fiber), 14g pro.

SALMON DILL SOUP

Rustic Fish Chowder

In my fish chowder, I use fresh halibut my brother-in-law, a commercial fisherman, catches in Kodiak, Alaska. Top off servings with grated Parmesan cheese, minced green onions or a few drops of hot sauce.
—*Diana Lassen, Eugene, OR*

- -

Prep: 15 min. • **Cook:** 30 min.
Makes: 12 servings

- ¼ cup butter, cubed
- 1 small onion, finely chopped
- 1 garlic clove, minced
- 3 lbs. potatoes (about 6 medium), cut into ½-in. cubes
- 1½ cups fresh or frozen corn
- 5 cups chicken broth
- 1½ tsp. salt
- ¾ tsp. celery salt
- ¾ tsp. pepper
- ½ tsp. dried thyme
- 1 lb. cod or halibut fillets, cut into ¾-in. pieces
- 1 cup heavy whipping cream

1. In a 6-qt. stockpot, heat the butter over medium heat. Add the onion; cook and stir 3-4 minutes or until tender. Add garlic; cook 1 minute longer. Add potatoes, corn, broth, salt, celery salt, pepper and thyme; bring to a boil. Reduce heat; simmer, covered, 10-15 minutes or until potatoes are tender. Mash potatoes slightly.

2. Stir in the cod and whipping cream; bring to a boil. Reduce the heat; simmer, covered, 6-8 minutes or until fish just begins to flake easily with a fork.

1 cup: 242 cal., 12g fat (7g sat. fat), 49mg chol., 842mg sod., 25g carb. (3g sugars, 3g fiber), 10g pro.

RUSTIC FISH CHOWDER

THAI
SHRIMP
SOUP

Thai Shrimp Soup

A potful of this delicious Thai-style soup comes together in mere minutes. I love the fact that the ingredients are available in my little local grocery store.
—*Jessie Grearson, Falmouth, ME*

- -

Prep: 20 min. • **Cook:** 20 min.
Makes: 8 servings

- 1   medium onion, chopped
- 1   Tbsp. olive oil
- 3   cups reduced-sodium chicken broth
- 1   cup water
- 1   Tbsp. brown sugar
- 1   Tbsp. minced fresh gingerroot
- 1   Tbsp. fish sauce or soy sauce
- 1   Tbsp. red curry paste
- 1   lemongrass stalk
- 1   lb. uncooked large shrimp, peeled and deveined
- 1½   cups frozen shelled edamame
- 1   can (13.66 oz.) light coconut milk
- 1   can (8¾ oz.) whole baby corn, drained and cut in half
- ½   cup bamboo shoots
- ¼   cup fresh basil leaves, julienned
- ¼   cup minced fresh cilantro
- 2   Tbsp. lime juice
- 1½   tsp. grated lime zest
- 1   tsp. curry powder

1. In a Dutch oven, saute onion in oil until tender. Add chicken broth, water, brown sugar, ginger, fish sauce, curry paste and lemongrass. Bring to a boil. Reduce heat; carefully stir in the shrimp and edamame. Cook, uncovered, for 5-6 minutes or until shrimp turn pink.

2. Add coconut milk, corn, bamboo shoots, basil, cilantro, lime juice, lime zest and curry powder; heat through. Discard lemongrass.

1 cup: 163 cal., 7g fat (3g sat. fat), 69mg chol., 505mg sod., 9g carb. (5g sugars, 2g fiber), 14g pro. **Diabetic exchanges:** 2 lean meat, 1 vegetable, 1 fat.

SHERRIED SWEET
POTATO SOUP, P. 74

Vegetarian & Meatless

Even meat lovers eat up every last spoonful of these deliciously satisfying soups and stews.

MOROCCAN
VEGETARIAN
STEW, P. 76

MUSHROOM & BROCCOLI SOUP

Spinach & Tortellini Soup

Stir cheese tortellini and fresh spinach into a simple tomato-enhanced broth. Delicious!
—*Debbie Wilson, Burlington, NC*

Takes: 20 min. • **Makes:** 6 servings

- 1 tsp. olive oil
- 2 garlic cloves, minced
- 1 can (14½ oz.) no-salt-added diced tomatoes, undrained
- 3 cans (14½ oz. each) vegetable broth
- 2 tsp. Italian seasoning
- 1 pkg. (9 oz.) refrigerated cheese tortellini
- 4 cups fresh baby spinach
  Shredded Parmesan cheese and freshly ground pepper

1. In a large saucepan, heat oil over medium heat. Add the garlic; cook and stir 1 minute. Stir in tomatoes, broth and Italian seasoning; bring to a boil. Add cheese tortellini; bring to a gentle boil. Cook, uncovered, just until tortellini are tender, 7-9 minutes.
2. Stir in the spinach. Sprinkle servings with cheese and pepper.

1⅓ cups: 164 cal., 5g fat (2g sat. fat), 18mg chol., 799mg sod., 25g carb. (4g sugars, 2g fiber), 7g pro.

Chili-Basil Tomato Soup

A co-worker shared her special soup recipe with my husband and me. Now it's a regular on our table alongside a tossed salad and a loaf of bread.
—*Penny Lund, Fort Collins, CO*

Takes: 20 min. • **Makes:** 6 servings

- 1 can (26 oz.) condensed tomato soup, undiluted
- 3 cups 2% milk
- 1 can (12 oz.) evaporated milk
- 1 can (10 oz.) diced tomatoes and green chiles, undrained
- 1 Tbsp. minced fresh basil or 1 tsp. dried basil
- ½ tsp. salt
- ¼ tsp. pepper
  Shredded Parmesan cheese, optional

In a Dutch oven, combine first 7 ingredients. Cook and stir over medium heat until heated through. Garnish servings with Parmesan cheese if desired.

1⅓ cups: 243 cal., 8g fat (5g sat. fat), 30mg chol., 1204mg sod., 33g carb. (23g sugars, 2g fiber), 10g pro.

Mushroom & Broccoli Soup

One of my daughters does not eat meat, while the other struggles to get enough fiber. Here's how I serve both of them a nutritious meal they're happy to have. I like to prepare the soup using leftover broccoli that I've saved and stored in the freezer.
—*Maria Davis, Flower Mound, TX*

Prep: 20 min. • **Cook:** 45 min.
Makes: 8 servings

- 1 bunch broccoli (about 1½ lbs.)
- 1 Tbsp. canola oil
- ½ lb. sliced fresh mushrooms
- 1 Tbsp. reduced-sodium soy sauce
- 2 medium carrots, finely chopped
- 2 celery ribs, finely chopped
- ¼ cup finely chopped onion
- 1 garlic clove, minced
- 1 carton (32 oz.) vegetable broth
- 2 cups water
- 2 Tbsp. lemon juice

1. Cut broccoli florets into bite-sized pieces. Peel and chop stalks.
2. In a large saucepan, heat the oil over medium-high heat; saute the mushrooms until tender, 4-6 minutes. Stir in soy sauce; remove from pan.
3. In same pan, combine broccoli stalks, carrots, celery, onion, garlic, broth and water; bring to a boil. Reduce heat; simmer, uncovered, until the vegetables are softened, 25-30 minutes.
4. Puree soup using an immersion blender. Or cool slightly and puree soup in a blender; return to pan. Stir in florets and mushrooms; bring to a boil. Reduce heat to medium; cook until broccoli is tender, 8-10 minutes, stirring occasionally. Stir in lemon juice.

¾ cup: 69 cal., 2g fat (0 sat. fat), 0 chol., 574mg sod., 11g carb. (4g sugars, 3g fiber), 4g pro. **Diabetic exchanges:** 2 vegetable, ½ fat.

SPINACH &
TORTELLINI SOUP

Hearty Quinoa & Corn Chowder

My grandmother lived in the Appalachian Mountains and cooked with the fresh-picked corn and beans from her garden. I updated her chowder by adding quinoa and herbs.
—Kari Napier, Louisville, KY

Prep: 25 min. + standing • **Cook:** 15 min.
Makes: 14 servings

- 3 medium sweet red peppers
- 1 cup quinoa, rinsed
- 1 Tbsp. butter
- 1 Tbsp. olive oil
- 1 medium onion, chopped
- 2 garlic cloves, minced
- ⅓ cup all-purpose flour
- 4 cups vegetable stock
- 2 cups heavy whipping cream
- 6 medium ears sweet corn, kernels removed (about 4 cups) or 2 pkg. (10 oz.) frozen corn, thawed
- 1 can (15 oz.) pinto beans, rinsed and drained
- 2 Tbsp. minced fresh parsley
- ½ tsp. minced fresh thyme
- 1½ tsp. salt
- ½ tsp. pepper

1. Broil peppers 4 in. from heat until skins blister, about 5 minutes. With tongs, rotate peppers a quarter turn. Broil and rotate until all sides are blistered and blackened. Immediately place peppers in a large bowl; cover and let stand for 20 minutes.
2. Peel off and discard charred skin. Remove stems and seeds. Finely chop peppers.
3. Meanwhile, in a Dutch oven, cook and stir the quinoa over medium-high heat for 3-5 minutes or until lightly toasted; remove from the pan.
4. In the same pan, heat butter and oil over medium-high heat. Add the onion; cook and stir until tender. Add garlic; cook 1 minute longer. Stir in flour until blended. Gradually whisk in stock and cream.
5. Add corn, beans, roasted peppers and quinoa; bring to a boil, stirring frequently. Reduce the heat; simmer, uncovered, for 15-20 minutes or until the quinoa is tender, stirring occasionally. Stir in the remaining ingredients.
¾ cup: 264 cal., 16g fat (9g sat. fat), 49mg chol., 485mg sod., 27g carb. (3g sugars, 4g fiber), 6g pro.

Sherried Sweet Potato Soup

When I want something out of the ordinary for my guests, I stir up a pot of spiced sweet potato soup. I use an immersion blender for a creamier texture.
—Charlene Chambers, Ormond Beach, FL

Prep: 15 min. • **Cook:** 45 min.
Makes: 8 servings

- 4 large sweet potatoes, peeled and cubed
- 1 small onion, chopped
- 2 Tbsp. butter
- 2 garlic cloves, minced
- 1 tsp. ground cumin
- ½ tsp. salt
- ½ tsp. minced fresh gingerroot
- ½ tsp. ground coriander
- ¼ tsp. ground cinnamon
- ⅛ tsp. ground cardamom
- 3 cans (14 oz. each) chicken broth
- 1 cup heavy whipping cream
- ⅓ cup sherry
- 1 Tbsp. lime juice
- 2 Tbsp. minced fresh cilantro

1. Place sweet potatoes in a large saucepan and cover with water. Bring to a boil. Reduce heat; cover and cook for 10-15 minutes or just until tender. Drain; set aside.
2. In a large saucepan, saute onion in butter until tender. Add garlic, cumin, salt, ginger, coriander, cinnamon and cardamom; cook for 2 minutes. Stir in potatoes and chicken broth; bring to a boil. Reduce heat; simmer, uncovered, for 25-30 minutes or until the flavors are blended.
3. Add whipping cream and sherry; bring to a boil. Reduce heat; simmer, uncovered, for 5 minutes. Remove from the heat; stir in the lime juice. Cool slightly. In a blender, process the soup in batches until smooth. Garnish with cilantro.
1 cup: 337 cal., 14g fat (9g sat. fat), 45mg chol., 903mg sod., 46g carb. (19g sugars, 6g fiber), 5g pro.

SHERRIED SWEET POTATO SOUP

VEGAN CABBAGE SOUP

Market Basket Soup

Enjoy a basketful of veggie taste! I make sure to include the kohlrabi. The addition of its mellow broccoli-cabbage flavor is wonderful.
—*Kellie Foglio, Salem, WI*

Prep: 25 min. • **Cook:** 40 min.
Makes: 11 servings

- 1 Tbsp. olive oil
- 1 large kohlrabi bulb, peeled and chopped
- 4 celery ribs, chopped
- 2 medium onions, chopped
- 2 medium carrots, chopped
- 3 garlic cloves, minced
- 1 tsp. salt
- 1 tsp. coarsely ground pepper
- 6 cups vegetable stock or water
- 2 cans (15½ oz. each) great northern beans, rinsed and drained
- 2 bay leaves
- 2 medium tomatoes, chopped
- 2 Tbsp. minced fresh parsley
- 2 Tbsp. minced fresh tarragon or ¾ tsp. dried tarragon
- 2 Tbsp. minced fresh thyme or ¾ tsp. dried thyme

1. In a stockpot, heat oil over medium-high heat. Stir in the kohlrabi, celery, onions and carrots; cook 5 minutes or until onions are softened. Add garlic, salt and pepper; cook and stir 5 minutes.
2. Stir in vegetable stock, beans and bay leaves. Bring to a boil over medium-high heat. Reduce heat; simmer, covered, until the vegetables are tender, 20-25 minutes. Add the remaining ingredients; simmer 5 minutes more. Discard bay leaves.
1 cup: 110 cal., 2g fat (0 sat. fat), 0 chol., 664mg sod., 19g carb. (3g sugars, 6g fiber), 5g pro. **Diabetic exchanges:** 1 starch, 1 vegetable.

Vegan Cabbage Soup

For an even heartier version of this delicious vegan choice, toss in canned beans, such as navy or cannellini.
—Taste of Home *Test Kitchen*

Prep: 15 min. • **Cook:** 6 hours
Makes: 10 servings

- 4 cups vegetable stock
- 1 can (14 oz.) Italian diced tomatoes
- 1 can (6 oz.) tomato paste
- 1 small head cabbage (about 1½ lbs.), shredded
- 4 celery ribs, chopped
- 2 large carrots, chopped
- 1 medium onion, chopped
- 2 garlic cloves, minced
- 2 tsp. Italian seasoning
- ½ tsp. salt
  Fresh basil, optional

In a 5- or 6-qt. slow cooker, whisk together the stock, diced tomatoes and tomato paste. Stir in vegetables, garlic, Italian seasoning and salt. Cook, covered, on low until the vegetables are tender, 6-8 hours. If desired, top with basil.
1 cup: 110 cal., 0 fat (0 sat. fat), 0 chol., 866mg sod., 24g carb. (13g sugars, 6g fiber), 4g pro.

Garlic Fennel Bisque

I usually serve this simple but special bisque as a springtime side dish or first course. The fennel is so refreshing.
—*Janet Ondrich, Thamesville, ON*

Prep: 30 min. • **Cook:** 40 min.
Makes: 14 servings

- 4 cups water
- 2½ cups half-and-half cream
- 24 garlic cloves, peeled and halved
- 3 medium fennel bulbs, cut into ½-in. pieces
- 2 Tbsp. chopped fennel fronds
- ½ tsp. salt
- ⅛ tsp. pepper
- ½ cup pine nuts, toasted

1. In a Dutch oven, bring the water, cream and garlic to a boil. Reduce heat; cover and simmer for 15 minutes or until garlic is very soft. Add the fennel and fennel fronds; cover and simmer 15 minutes longer or until fennel is very soft.
2. Cool slightly. In a blender, process soup in batches until blended. Return all to pan. Season with salt and pepper; heat through. Sprinkle each serving with pine nuts.
½ cup: 108 cal., 7g fat (3g sat. fat), 21mg chol., 133mg sod., 8g carb. (2g sugars, 2g fiber), 4g pro.

MOROCCAN
VEGETARIAN
STEW

GOLDEN BEET
& PEACH SOUP
WITH TARRAGON

Moroccan Vegetarian Stew

Serve this fragrant, spicy stew over couscous
or with pita bread. A dollop of yogurt or sour
cream on top makes a cool contrast.
—*Sonya Labbe, West Hollywood, CA*

Prep: 20 min. • **Cook:** 30 min.
Makes: 8 servings

- 1   Tbsp. olive oil
- 1   large onion, chopped
- 2   tsp. ground cumin
- 2   tsp. ground cinnamon
- 1   tsp. ground coriander
- ½   tsp. ground allspice
- ½   tsp. cayenne pepper
- ¼   tsp. salt
- 1   small butternut squash, peeled and
       cut into 1-in. cubes (about 4 cups)
- 2   medium potatoes, peeled and cut
       into 1-in. cubes (about 4 cups)
- 4   medium carrots, sliced
- 3   plum tomatoes, chopped
- 3   cups water
- 2   small zucchini, cut into 1-in. cubes
- 1   can (15 oz.) garbanzo beans
       or chickpeas, rinsed and drained

1. In a 6-qt. stockpot, heat the olive oil over
medium-high heat; saute onion until tender.
Add seasonings; cook and stir 1 minute.
2. Stir in the squash, potatoes, carrots,
tomatoes and water; bring to a boil. Reduce
heat; simmer, uncovered, until squash and
potatoes are almost tender, 15-20 minutes.
3. Add the zucchini and beans; bring to a boil.
Reduce heat; simmer, uncovered, until the
vegetables are tender, 5-8 minutes.
1½ cups: 180 cal., 3g fat (0 sat. fat), 0 chol.,
174mg sod., 36g carb. (8g sugars, 9g fiber),
5g pro. **Diabetic exchanges:** 2 starch,
1 vegetable.

Golden Beet & Peach Soup with Tarragon

One summer our two peach trees yielded a bumper crop, and I had fun experimenting in the kitchen. After finding a recipe for beet soup, I changed it to include our homegrown golden beets and sweet peaches.
—*Sue Gronholz, Beaver Dam, WI*

Prep: 20 min. • **Bake:** 40 min. + chilling
Makes: 6 servings

- 2 lbs. fresh golden beets, peeled and cut into 1-in. cubes
- 1 Tbsp. olive oil
- 2 cups white grape-peach juice
- 2 Tbsp. cider vinegar
- ¼ cup plain Greek yogurt
- ¼ tsp. finely chopped fresh tarragon
- 2 medium fresh peaches, peeled and diced
  Fresh tarragon sprigs

1. Preheat oven to 400°. Place the beets in a 15x10x1-in. baking pan. Drizzle with olive oil; toss to coat. Roast until tender, 40-45 minutes. Cool slightly.
2. Transfer the beets to a blender or food processor. Add juice and vinegar; process until smooth. Refrigerate at least 1 hour. In a small bowl, combine Greek yogurt and chopped tarragon; refrigerate.
3. To serve, divide the beet mixture among individual bowls; place a spoonful of yogurt mixture in each bowl. Top with diced peaches and tarragon sprigs.

⅔ cup: 159 cal., 4g fat (1g sat. fat), 3mg chol., 129mg sod., 31g carb. (26g sugars, 4g fiber), 3g pro. **Diabetic exchanges:** 2 vegetable, 1 fruit, ½ fat.

 TIP

If you'd like, blend the tarragon—or the herb of your choice—with the beets instead of with the plain Greek yogurt.

Coconut Red Curry Stew

This bright, aromatic stew is brimming with nutritious goodness and bold flavors. I like mine best with sticky rice.
—Marly Chaland, Maple, ON

Prep: 20 min. • **Cook:** 50 min.
Makes: 4 servings

- 1 Tbsp. canola oil
- 1 medium onion, chopped
- 1 garlic clove, minced
- 3 to 4 Tbsp. red curry paste
- ½ tsp. sugar
- 1 small eggplant, cut into 1-in. pieces (about 4 cups)
- 3 cups cubed peeled butternut squash (1 in.)
- 1 medium sweet red pepper, cut into 1-in. pieces
- 1 medium green pepper, cut into 1-in. pieces
- 1 can (15 oz.) garbanzo beans or chickpeas, rinsed and drained
- 1 carton (32 oz.) vegetable broth, divided
- 1 can (15 oz.) crushed tomatoes
- 1 can (13.66 oz.) coconut milk
  Chopped fresh cilantro
  Optional: Lime wedges and hot cooked rice

1. In a 6-qt. stockpot, heat the oil over medium-high heat; saute onion until lightly browned, 3-4 minutes. Add garlic; cook and stir 1 minute. Stir in curry paste and sugar.
2. Stir in vegetables, garbanzo beans, 3 cups broth, tomatoes and coconut milk; bring to a boil. Reduce heat; simmer, covered, until the vegetables are tender, 35-40 minutes.
3. Stir in the remaining broth; heat through. Serve with cilantro and, if desired, lime wedges and rice.
1½ cups: 457 cal., 22g fat (16g sat. fat), 0 chol., 1364mg sod., 59g carb. (20g sugars, 14g fiber), 11g pro.

TACO TWIST SOUP

Taco Twist Soup

The fun, family-friendly twist in this taco soup is the spiral pasta. I lightened up the original recipe a bit by replacing the ground beef with black beans.
—Colleen Zertler, Menomonie, WI

Takes: 30 min. • **Makes:** 6 servings

- 2 tsp. olive oil
- 1 medium onion, chopped
- 2 garlic cloves, minced
- 3 cups vegetable broth or reduced-sodium beef broth
- 1 can (15 oz.) black beans, rinsed and drained
- 1 can (14½ oz.) diced tomatoes, undrained
- 1½ cups picante sauce
- 1 cup uncooked spiral pasta
- 1 small green pepper, chopped
- 2 tsp. chili powder
- 1 tsp. ground cumin
  Optional toppings: Shredded cheddar cheese, sour cream and cilantro

1. In a large saucepan, heat the oil over medium-high heat. Add onion and garlic; cook and stir until crisp-tender, 3-4 minutes.
2. Stir in broth, beans, tomatoes, picante sauce, pasta, green pepper and seasonings. Bring to a boil, stirring frequently. Reduce heat; cover and simmer until the pasta is tender, 10-12 minutes, stirring occasionally. If desired, serve with optional toppings.
1 cup: 176 cal., 2g fat (0 sat. fat), 0 chol., 1044mg sod., 32g carb. (7g sugars, 5g fiber), 7g pro.

Caribbean Potato Soup

Take your taste buds to a tropical paradise with a mouthwatering medley of Caribbean ingredients. No kale on hand? Feel free to substitute fresh spinach.
—*Crystal Jo Bruns, Iliff, CO*

Takes: 30 min. • **Makes:** 6 servings

- 2 medium onions, chopped
- 2 tsp. canola oil
- 3 garlic cloves, minced
- 2 tsp. minced fresh gingerroot
- 2 tsp. ground coriander
- 1 tsp. ground turmeric
- ½ tsp. dried thyme
- ¼ tsp. ground allspice
- 5 cups vegetable broth
- 2 cups cubed peeled sweet potato
- 3 cups chopped fresh kale
- 1 cup frozen sliced okra
- 1 cup coconut milk
- 1 cup canned diced tomatoes, drained
- 1 cup canned black-eyed peas, rinsed and drained
- 2 Tbsp. lime juice

1. In a Dutch oven, saute onions in oil until tender. Add the garlic, ginger and spices; cook 1 minute longer.
2. Stir in vegetable broth and potato. Bring to a boil. Reduce heat; cover and simmer for 5 minutes. Stir in kale and okra. Return to a boil; cover and simmer 10 minutes longer or until potato is tender. Add coconut milk, tomatoes, peas and lime juice; heat through.
1½ cups: 213 cal., 10g fat (7g sat. fat), 0 chol., 954mg sod., 28g carb. (9g sugars, 6g fiber), 5g pro.

CARIBBEAN POTATO SOUP

Over-the-Rainbow Minestrone

Anyone who loves minestrone won't want to miss this one. With a rainbow of veggies, it definitely lives up to its name.
—*Crystal Schlueter, Northglenn, CO*

Prep: 20 min. • **Cook:** 6 hours 20 minutes
Makes: 10 servings

- 4 large stems Swiss chard (about ½ lb.) or fresh baby spinach
- 2 Tbsp. olive oil
- 1 medium red onion, finely chopped
- 6 cups vegetable broth
- 2 cans (14½ oz. each) fire-roasted diced tomatoes, undrained
- 1 can (16 oz.) kidney beans, rinsed and drained
- 1 can (15 oz.) garbanzo beans or chickpeas, rinsed and drained
- 1 medium yellow summer squash or zucchini, halved and cut into ¼-in. slices
- 1 medium sweet red or yellow pepper, finely chopped
- 1 medium carrot, finely chopped
- 2 garlic cloves, minced
- 1½ cups uncooked spiral pasta or small pasta shells
- ¼ cup prepared pesto
  Optional toppings: Additional prepared pesto, shredded Parmesan cheese, crushed red pepper flakes and minced fresh basil

1. Cut stems from chard; chop stems and leaves separately. Reserve leaves for adding later. In a large skillet, heat oil over medium heat. Add the onion and chard stems; cook and stir 3-5 minutes or until tender. Transfer to a 6-qt. slow cooker.
2. Stir in vegetable broth, tomatoes, kidney beans, garbanzo beans, squash, pepper, carrot and garlic. Cook, covered, on low 6-8 hours or until vegetables are tender.
3. Stir in spiral pasta and reserved chard leaves. Cook, covered, on low 20-25 minutes longer or until the pasta is tender; stir in the pesto. If desired, serve with additional pesto, Parmesan cheese, red pepper flakes and fresh basil.
1½ cups: 231 cal., 7g fat (1g sat. fat), 2mg chol., 1015mg sod., 34g carb. (7g sugars, 6g fiber), 9g pro.

SPRING ESSENCE SOUP
WITH PISTOU, P. 89

Healthy & Light

Crave-worthy soups and stews can fit into a special diet or eating plan—it's true. Here's proof!

LEMON CHICKEN & RICE SOUP, P. 87

Cool as a Cucumber Soup

Here's a wonderful side dish or appetizer for hot summer days. Bursts of dill contrast so well with the milder cucumber flavor.
—*Deirdre Cox, Kansas City, MO*

Prep: 15 min. + standing • **Makes:** 5 servings

- 1 lb. cucumbers, peeled, seeded and sliced
- ½ tsp. salt
- 1½ cups fat-free plain yogurt
- 1 green onion, coarsely chopped
- 1 garlic clove, minced
- 4½ tsp. snipped fresh dill
  Additional chopped green onion and snipped fresh dill

1. In a colander set over a bowl, toss the cucumber slices with salt. Let stand for 30 minutes. Squeeze and pat dry.
2. Place the cucumbers, yogurt, onion and garlic in a food processor; cover and process until smooth. Stir in dill. Serve immediately in chilled bowls. Garnish with additional onion and dill.
⅔ cup: 40 cal., 0 fat (0 sat. fat), 2mg chol., 279mg sod., 8g carb. (5g sugars, 1g fiber), 3g pro. **Diabetic exchanges:** ½ fat-free milk.

Texas Black Bean Soup

I love being able to toss convenient canned items into the slow cooker and then lifting the lid later to find a heartwarming meal.
—*Pamela Scott, Garland, TX*

Prep: 5 min. • **Cook:** 4 hours
Makes: 10 servings

- 2 cans (15 oz. each) black beans, rinsed and drained
- 1 can (14½ oz.) stewed tomatoes or Mexican stewed tomatoes, cut up
- 1 can (14½ oz.) diced tomatoes or diced tomatoes with green chiles
- 1 can (14½ oz.) chicken broth
- 1 can (11 oz.) Mexicorn, drained
- 2 cans (4 oz. each) chopped green chiles
- 4 green onions, thinly sliced
- 2 to 3 Tbsp. chili powder
- 1 tsp. ground cumin
- ½ tsp. dried minced garlic

In a 3-qt. slow cooker, combine all ingredients. Cover and cook on high for 4-6 hours or until heated through.
1 cup: 91 cal., 0 fat (0 sat. fat), 0 chol., 609mg sod., 19g carb. (6g sugars, 4g fiber), 4g pro.

SPICY PERUVIAN POTATO SOUP

Spicy Peruvian Potato Soup

This robust Peruvian soup (*locro de papas*) has the comfort of potatoes and the spiciness of chiles. Light enough for a casual lunch, a bowlful is also satisfying enough to serve as a main course for dinner.
—Taste of Home *Test Kitchen*

Prep: 35 min. • **Cook:** 4 hours
Makes: 8 servings

- 1 Tbsp. olive oil
- 1 medium onion, chopped
- 1 medium sweet red pepper, cut into 1-in. pieces
- 3 garlic cloves, minced
- 1 carton (32 oz.) chicken stock
- 2 large Yukon Gold potatoes, peeled and cut into 1-in. cubes
- 1 can (4 oz.) chopped green chiles
- ½ cup minced fresh cilantro, divided
- ½ to 1 serrano pepper, seeded and finely chopped
- 2 tsp. ground cumin
- 1 tsp. dried oregano
- ¼ tsp. salt
- ¼ tsp. pepper
- 1 fully cooked Spanish chorizo link (3 oz.), chopped
  Optional toppings: Sour cream and cubed avocado

1. In a large skillet, heat oil over medium-high heat. Add the onion and sweet pepper; cook and stir until crisp-tender, 6-8 minutes. Add the garlic; cook 1 minute longer. Transfer to a 4- or 5-qt. slow cooker. Add the stock, potatoes, chiles, ¼ cup cilantro, serrano pepper and seasonings. Cook, covered, on low until potatoes are tender, 4-6 hours.
2. Remove the soup from heat; cool slightly. Process in batches in a blender until smooth. Return to the slow cooker. Stir in the chorizo and remaining ¼ cup cilantro; heat through. If desired, serve with sour cream and cubed avocado.
1 cup: 153 cal., 5g fat (1g sat. fat), 7mg chol., 472mg sod., 23g carb. (3g sugars, 2g fiber), 6g pro. **Diabetic exchanges:** 1½ starch, 1 fat.

Homemade Apple Cider Beef Stew

In fall when the air gets crisp and Nebraska's orchards start selling fresh cider, I simmer my tangy beef stew. Its subtle sweetness is a delightful change from other versions. We round out the meal with biscuits and slices of apple and cheddar cheese.
—*Joyce Glaesemann, Lincoln, NE*

Prep: 30 min. • **Cook:** 1¾ hours
Makes: 8 servings

- 2   lbs. beef stew meat, cut into 1-in. cubes
- 2   Tbsp. canola oil
- 3   cups apple cider or juice
- 1   can (14½ oz.) reduced-sodium beef broth
- 2   Tbsp. cider vinegar
- 1½ tsp. salt
- ¼ to ½ tsp. dried thyme
- ¼   tsp. pepper
- 3   medium potatoes, peeled and cubed
- 4   medium carrots, cut into ¾-in. pieces
- 3   celery ribs, cut into ¾-in. pieces
- 2   medium onions, cut into wedges
- ¼   cup all-purpose flour
- ¼   cup water
      Fresh thyme sprigs, optional

1. In a Dutch oven, brown beef on all sides in oil over medium-high heat; drain. Add the cider, beef broth, vinegar, salt, thyme and pepper; bring to a boil. Reduce heat; cover and simmer for 1¼ hours.
2. Add the potatoes, carrots, celery and onions; return to a boil. Reduce heat; cover and simmer for 30-35 minutes or until beef and vegetables are tender.
3. Combine flour and water until smooth; stir into stew. Bring to a boil; cook and stir for 2 minutes or until thickened. If desired, serve with fresh thyme.
1 cup: 330 cal., 12g fat (3g sat. fat), 72mg chol., 628mg sod., 31g carb. (14g sugars, 2g fiber), 24g pro. **Diabetic exchanges:** 3 lean meat, 1½ starch, 1 vegetable.

Turkey Ginger Noodle Soup

I wanted something comforting yet healthy, and ginger is my favorite spice. This recipe was a must-try, and it didn't disappoint!
—*Adina Monson, Nanaimo, BC*

Prep: 20 min. • **Cook:** 4¼ hours
Makes: 8 servings

- 2   medium carrots, sliced
- 2   cans (8 oz. each) sliced water chestnuts, drained
- 3 to 4 Tbsp. minced fresh gingerroot
- 2   Tbsp. minced fresh parsley
- 2   tsp. chili powder
- 1   carton (32 oz.) chicken stock
- 1   can (11.8 oz.) coconut water
- 3   Tbsp. lemon juice
- 2   lbs. uncooked skinless turkey breast, cut into 1-in. cubes
- 2   tsp. pepper
- ½   tsp. salt
- 2   Tbsp. canola oil
- 1   cup frozen corn (about 5 oz.), thawed
- 1   cup frozen peas (about 4 oz.), thawed
- 8   oz. rice noodles or thin spaghetti

1. Place the first 8 ingredients in a 4- or 5-qt. slow cooker.
2. Toss turkey with pepper and salt. In a large skillet, heat the oil over medium-high heat; brown turkey in batches. Add to slow cooker.
3. Cook, covered, on low until carrots and turkey are tender, 4-5 hours. Stir in corn and peas; heat through.
4. Cook the rice noodles according to the package directions; drain. Add to soup just before serving.
1½ cups: 351 cal., 6g fat (1g sat. fat), 65mg chol., 672mg sod., 41g carb. (5g sugars, 4g fiber), 33g pro. **Diabetic exchanges:** 3 starch, 3 lean meat.

HOMEMADE
APPLE CIDER
BEEF STEW

Carrot Ginger Soup

Fresh ginger makes a big difference in this simple but special vegan choice. Bright and flavorful, it comes together easily yet always impresses guests. I tightly wrap any extra soup and store it in the freezer to pull out whenever I have a craving.
—*Jenna Olson, Manchester, MO*

Take: 30 min..
Makes: 4 servings

- 1 **Tbsp. olive oil**
- 1 **small onion, chopped**
- 1 **garlic clove, minced**
- 3 **tsp. minced fresh gingerroot**
- 4 **large carrots, peeled and chopped**
- 3 **cups vegetable broth**
- 2 **tsp. grated lemon zest**
- ½ **tsp. salt**
- ¼ **tsp. ground black pepper**
- 2 **Tbsp. fresh lemon juice**
  Additional lemon zest, optional

In a Dutch oven or stockpot, heat oil over medium heat. Add onion; cook and stir until tender, 4-5 minutes. Add garlic and ginger; cook 1 minute longer. Stir in carrots, broth, zest, salt and pepper; bring to a boil. Reduce heat; simmer, covered, until carrots are tender, 10-12 minutes. Pulse mixture in a blender or with an immersion blender until desired consistency; stir in lemon juice. If desired, garnish with additional lemon zest.
Freeze option: Cool soup; freeze in freezer containers. To use, partially thaw soup in the refrigerator overnight. Heat through in a large saucepan over medium-low heat, stirring occasionally; add a little broth or water if necessary.
1¾ cup: 80 cal., 4g fat (1g sat. fat), 0 chol., 551mg sod., 11g carb. (5g sugars, 2g fiber), 1g pro. **Diabetic exchanges:** 2 vegetable, 1 fat.

CARROT GINGER SOUP

GROUND BEEF VEGGIE STEW

Ground Beef Veggie Stew

Wondering what to do with an abundance of garden veggies? Put sweet red pepper, zucchini and yellow summer squash to good use in a hearty ground beef stew. I like that it's not only a filling meal but also a perfect addition to a healthier eating plan.
—*Courtney Stultz, Weir, KS*

- -

Takes: 30 min.
Makes: 6 servings

1   lb. lean ground beef (90% lean)
1   Tbsp. olive oil
1   small yellow summer squash, chopped
1   small zucchini, chopped
1   small sweet red pepper, chopped
2   cans (15 oz. each) diced tomatoes
1   cup water
1   tsp. salt
¼   tsp. pepper
3   Tbsp. minced fresh cilantro
    Reduced-fat sour cream, optional

1. In a large saucepan, cook ground beef over medium-high heat until no longer pink, 5-7 minutes, breaking into crumbles; drain. Remove from pan; set aside.
2. In the same saucepan, add the oil, squash, zucchini and red pepper; cook and stir until crisp-tender, 5-7 minutes. Add the ground beef, tomatoes, water, salt and pepper; bring to a boil. Reduce to a simmer; cook, stirring occasionally, until the vegetables are tender, 5-8 minutes. Stir in minced cilantro to serve. If desired, top with sour cream.

1¼ cups: 180 cal., 9g fat (3g sat. fat), 47mg chol., 663mg sod., 9g carb. (6g sugars, 3g fiber), 16g pro. **Diabetic exchanges:** 2 lean meat, 1 vegetable, ½ fat.

TIP

If you're not a fan of cilantro, try replacing it in this savory beef stew with chopped fresh chives or parsley.

Chicken Mushroom Stew

The flavors blend beautifully in this chunky stew as the chicken, vegetables and herbs simmer together in the slow cooker. What a treat at the end of a busy day!
—*Kenny Van Rheenen, Mendota, IL*

Prep: 20 min. • **Cook:** 4 hours
Makes: 6 servings

- 6 boneless skinless chicken breast halves (4 oz. each)
- 2 Tbsp. canola oil, divided
- 8 oz. fresh mushrooms, sliced
- 1 medium onion, diced
- 3 cups diced zucchini
- 1 cup chopped green pepper
- 4 garlic cloves, minced
- 3 medium tomatoes, chopped
- 1 can (6 oz.) tomato paste
- ¾ cup water
- 2 tsp. each dried thyme, oregano, marjoram and basil
  Chopped fresh thyme, optional

1. Cut chicken into 1-in. cubes; brown in 1 Tbsp. oil in a large skillet. Transfer to a 3-qt. slow cooker. In the same skillet, saute mushrooms, onion, zucchini and green pepper in remaining oil until crisp-tender; add garlic; cook 1 minute longer.
2. Place in slow cooker. Add the tomatoes, tomato paste, water and seasonings. Cover and cook on low for 4-5 hours or until meat is no longer pink and vegetables are tender. If desired, top with chopped fresh thyme.
1⅓ cups: 237 cal., 8g fat (1g sat. fat), 63mg chol., 82mg sod., 15g carb. (7g sugars, 3g fiber), 27g pro. **Diabetic exchanges:** 3 lean meat, 1 starch, 1 fat.

CAROLINA SHRIMP SOUP

Carolina Shrimp Soup

Fresh shrimp from the Carolina coast is one of our favorite foods. We toss it into broth along with kale, garlic, black-eyed peas and a red pepper to make a wholesome meal.
—*Mary Leverette, Columbia, SC*

Takes: 25 min. • **Makes:** 6 servings

- 4 tsp. olive oil, divided
- 1 lb. uncooked shrimp (31-40 per lb.), peeled and deveined
- 5 garlic cloves, minced
- 1 bunch kale, trimmed and coarsely chopped (about 16 cups)
- 1 medium sweet red pepper, cut into ¾-in. pieces
- 3 cups reduced-sodium chicken broth
- 1 can (15½ oz.) black-eyed peas, rinsed and drained
- ¼ tsp. salt
- ¼ tsp. pepper
  Minced fresh chives, optional

1. In a 6-qt. stockpot, heat 2 tsp. oil over medium-high heat. Add the shrimp; cook and stir 2 minutes. Add the garlic; cook just until shrimp turn pink, 1-2 minutes longer. Remove from pot.
2. In same pot, heat the remaining oil over medium-high heat. Stir in the kale and red pepper; cook, covered, until kale is tender, stirring occasionally, 8-10 minutes. Add the broth; bring to a boil. Stir in the peas, salt, pepper and shrimp; heat through. If desired, sprinkle each serving with chives.
1 cup: 188 cal., 5g fat (1g sat. fat), 92mg chol., 585mg sod., 18g carb. (2g sugars, 3g fiber), 19g pro. **Diabetic exchanges:** 2 lean meat, 2 vegetable, ½ starch, ½ fat.

Lemon Chicken & Rice Soup

Years ago, I fell in love with a special menu item at Panera Bread—a lemony Greek soup. I couldn't wait to re-create it at home. Now we can have my version any time we want.
—*Kristin Cherry, Bothell, WA*

Prep: 35 min. • **Cook:** 4¼ hours
Makes: 12 servings

- 2 Tbsp. olive oil
- 2 lbs. boneless skinless chicken breasts, cut into ½-in. pieces
- 5 cans (14½ oz. each) reduced-sodium chicken broth
- 8 cups coarsely chopped Swiss chard, kale or spinach
- 2 large carrots, finely chopped
- 1 small onion, chopped
- 1 medium lemon, halved and thinly sliced
- ¼ cup lemon juice
- 4 tsp. grated lemon zest
- ½ tsp. pepper
- 4 cups cooked brown rice

1. In a large skillet, heat 1 Tbsp. oil over medium-high heat. Add half of the chicken; cook and stir until browned. Transfer to a 6-qt. slow cooker. Repeat with remaining oil and chicken.
2. Stir broth, vegetables, lemon slices, lemon juice, lemon zest and pepper into chicken. Cook, covered, on low until chicken is tender, 4-5 hours. Stir in rice; heat through.
1⅓ cups: 203 cal., 5g fat (1g sat. fat), 42mg chol., 612mg sod., 20g carb. (3g sugars, 2g fiber), 20g pro. **Diabetic exchanges:** 2 lean meat, 1 starch, 1 vegetable, ½ fat.

LEMON CHICKEN & RICE SOUP

Fresh Asparagus Soup

We grow a lot of asparagus and like to use it in a variety of ways. Its refreshing taste really comes through in this simple recipe. Sometimes I'll heat up a serving in a coffee mug for an afternoon snack.
—*Sherri Melotik, Oak Creek, WI*

Prep: 15 min. • **Cook:** 20 min.
Makes: 6 servings

- 1 tsp. canola oil
- 1 small onion, chopped
- 1 garlic clove, minced
- 2 lbs. fresh asparagus, trimmed and cut into 1-in. pieces (about 5 cups)
- 1 can (14½ oz.) reduced-sodium chicken broth
- 4 Tbsp. all-purpose flour, divided
- 2½ cups fat-free milk, divided
- 2 Tbsp. butter
- ¾ tsp. salt
- ⅛ tsp. dried thyme
- ⅛ tsp. pepper
- ½ cup half-and-half cream
- 2 Tbsp. white wine
- 1 Tbsp. lemon juice
  Minced fresh chives, optional

1. In a large saucepan, heat oil over medium heat. Add onion; cook and stir 4-6 minutes or until tender. Add garlic; cook 1 minute longer. Add asparagus and broth; bring to a boil. Reduce heat; simmer, uncovered, 8-10 minutes or until asparagus is tender. Remove from heat; cool slightly. Transfer to a blender; cover and process until smooth.
2. In a small bowl, mix 2 Tbsp. flour and ¼ cup milk until smooth; set aside. In same saucepan, heat butter over medium heat. Stir in seasonings and remaining flour until smooth; cook and stir 45-60 seconds or until light golden brown. Gradually whisk in the cream, remaining milk and reserved flour mixture. Bring to a boil, stirring constantly; cook and stir 1-2 minutes or until thickened. Stir in the wine, lemon juice and asparagus mixture; heat through. If desired, top each serving with chives.
1 cup: 154 cal., 7g fat (4g sat. fat), 22mg chol., 585mg sod., 15g carb. (8g sugars, 2g fiber), 8g pro. **Diabetic exchanges:** 1½ fat, 1 vegetable, ½ fat-free milk.

SPRING ESSENCE
SOUP WITH PISTOU

Spring Essence Soup with Pistou

Near the end of April, I decided to go out and pick everything I could find in my vegetable garden—asparagus, rhubarb, oregano and leeks. This seasonal selection became the base for my spring essence soup. It's truly a layering of flavors.
—*Laurie Bock, Lynden, WA*

Prep: 20 min. • **Cook:** 25 min.
Makes: 6 servings

- 1 medium leek (white portion only), cut into ¼-in. slices
- 1 large carrot, chopped
- 1 small sweet red pepper, chopped
- 1 Tbsp. olive oil
- 2 garlic cloves, minced
- 4 cups chicken stock
- 10 baby red potatoes, quartered
- 6 fresh asparagus spears, cut into 1-in. pieces
- 1 cup chopped fresh rhubarb
- 1 tsp. sugar
- ½ tsp. salt
- ¼ tsp. pepper

PISTOU
- ½ cup loosely packed fresh oregano
- 2 Tbsp. chopped hazelnuts, toasted
- 1½ tsp. olive oil
- ½ tsp. minced garlic
- ⅛ tsp. salt

1. In a large saucepan, saute the leek, carrot and red pepper in oil until crisp-tender. Add the garlic; cook 1 minute longer. Stir in stock and potatoes. Bring to a boil. Reduce heat; cover and simmer for 5 minutes. Stir in the asparagus, rhubarb, sugar, salt and pepper; cover and simmer 4-6 minutes longer or until vegetables are tender.
2. Meanwhile, place the oregano, hazelnuts, oil, garlic and salt in a food processor; cover and pulse until blended. Serve with soup.
1 cup with 1 tsp. pistou: 147 cal., 5g fat (1g sat. fat), 0 chol., 601mg sod., 21g carb. (4g sugars, 3g fiber), 6g pro.

 TIP

Once you make pistou, you'll want it all the time! Try this distinctive sauce over your favorite pasta or grilled chicken.

MEDITERRANEAN
CHICKEN ORZO SOUP

Mediterranean Chicken Orzo Soup

My husband is Greek, and I'm always on the lookout for new Mediterranean specialties to try. Of all the recipes I've made, this is his favorite. Serve it with a little feta or Parmesan cheese and a side of toast.
—*Kristine Kosturos, Olympia, WA*

Prep: 20 min. • **Cook:** 25 min.
Makes: 6 servings

- 2 Tbsp. olive oil, divided
- ¾ lb. boneless skinless chicken breasts, cubed
- 2 celery ribs, chopped
- 2 medium carrots, chopped
- 1 small onion, chopped
- ½ tsp. salt
- ½ tsp. dried oregano
- ¼ tsp. pepper
- ¼ cup white wine or additional reduced-sodium chicken broth
- 1 carton (32 oz.) reduced-sodium chicken broth
- 1 tsp. minced fresh rosemary
- 1 bay leaf
- 1 cup uncooked whole wheat orzo pasta
- 1 tsp. grated lemon zest
- 1 Tbsp. lemon juice
  Minced fresh parsley, optional

1. In a large saucepan, heat 1 Tbsp. oil over medium-high heat. Add the chicken; cook and stir 6-8 minutes or until no longer pink. Remove from pan.
2. In the same pan, heat the remaining oil over medium-high heat. Add the vegetables, salt, oregano and pepper; cook and stir 4-6 minutes or until the vegetables are crisp-tender. Add wine, stirring to loosen browned bits from pan. Stir in chicken broth, rosemary and bay leaf; bring to a boil.
3. Add orzo. Reduce heat; simmer, covered, 15-18 minutes or until orzo is tender, stirring occasionally. Return the chicken to pan; heat through. Stir in lemon zest and lemon juice; remove bay leaf. If desired, top each serving with parsley.
1⅔ cups: 223 cal., 6g fat (1g sat. fat), 31mg chol., 630mg sod., 23g carb. (2g sugars, 5g fiber), 17g pro. **Diabetic exchanges:** 2 lean meat, 1 starch, 1 vegetable, 1 fat.

MEATBALL
ALPHABET SOUP, P. 97

Pasta & Noodles

Oodles of egg noodles, alphabet pasta, bow ties and more are waiting for you—by the bowlful!

LEMONY CHICKEN
NOODLE SOUP, P. 94

Lentil & Pasta Stew

Warm up body and soul with a big helping of this stick-to-your-ribs stew. Loaded with chopped smoked sausage, veggies and lentils, it's terrific with fresh-baked bread.
—*Geraldine Saucier, Albuquerque, NM*

Prep: 25 min. • **Cook:** 8 hours
Makes: 8 servings

- ½ lb. smoked kielbasa or Polish sausage, chopped
- 3 Tbsp. olive oil
- 3 Tbsp. butter
- 1 cup cubed peeled potatoes
- ¾ cup sliced fresh carrots
- 1 celery rib, sliced
- 1 small onion, finely chopped
- 5 cups beef broth
- 1 cup dried lentils, rinsed
- 1 cup canned diced tomatoes
- 1 bay leaf
- 1 tsp. coarsely ground pepper
- ¼ tsp. salt
- 1 cup uncooked ditalini or other small pasta
  Shredded Romano cheese

1. Brown kielbasa in oil and butter in a large skillet. Add the potatoes, carrots, celery and onion. Cook and stir for 3 minutes over medium heat. Transfer to a 4- or 5-qt. slow cooker. Stir in the broth, lentils, tomatoes, bay leaf, pepper and salt.
2. Cover and cook on low for 8-10 hours or until the lentils are tender. Cook the pasta according to the package directions; drain. Stir pasta into slow cooker. Discard bay leaf. Sprinkle servings with cheese.
1 cup: 364 cal., 18g fat (6g sat. fat), 30mg chol., 1021mg sod., 36g carb. (3g sugars, 9g fiber), 15g pro.

 TIP

When you need to bring a dish to a fall or winter get-together, this chunky stew is a great choice. Simply transport it in the slow cooker in which it was prepared, wrapping rubber bands around the handles and lid to secure the lid in place. (Don't forget the extension cord!)

CREAMY CHICKEN GNOCCHI SOUP

Creamy Chicken Gnocchi Soup

I tasted a similar soup at Olive Garden and wanted to see if I could re-create it myself at home. Here's the result! I love being able to enjoy it any time the mood strikes.
—*Jaclynn Robinson, Shingletown, CA*

Prep: 25 min. • **Cook:** 15 min.
Makes: 8 servings

- 1 lb. boneless skinless chicken breasts, cut into ½-in. pieces
- ⅓ cup butter, divided
- 1 small onion, chopped
- 1 medium carrot, shredded
- 1 celery rib, chopped
- 2 garlic cloves, minced
- ⅓ cup all-purpose flour
- 3½ cups 2% milk
- 1½ cups heavy whipping cream
- 1 Tbsp. reduced-sodium chicken bouillon granules
- ¼ tsp. coarsely ground pepper
- 1 pkg. (16 oz.) potato gnocchi
- ½ cup chopped fresh spinach

1. In a Dutch oven, brown chicken in 2 Tbsp. butter. Remove and keep warm. In the same pan, saute onion, carrot, celery and garlic in remaining butter until tender.
2. Whisk in flour until blended; gradually stir in milk, cream, bouillon and pepper. Bring to a boil. Reduce heat; cook and stir until thickened, about 2 minutes.
3. Add the gnocchi and spinach; cook until spinach is wilted, 3-4 minutes. Add chicken. Cover and simmer until heated through (do not boil), about 10 minutes.
1 cup: 482 cal., 28g fat (17g sat. fat), 125mg chol., 527mg sod., 36g carb. (10g sugars, 2g fiber), 21g pro.

LENTIL &
PASTA STEW

Lemony Chicken Noodle Soup

This isn't Grandma's chicken soup—but it's just as comforting! The splash of lemon juice adds a refreshing twist.
—*Bill Hilbrich, St. Cloud, MN*

Takes: 30 min. • **Makes:** 2 servings

- 1 small onion, chopped
- 2 Tbsp. olive oil
- 1 Tbsp. butter
- ¼ lb. boneless skinless chicken breast, cubed
- 1 garlic clove, minced
- 2 cans (14½ oz. each) chicken broth
- 1 medium carrot, cut into ¼-in. slices
- ¼ cup fresh or frozen peas
- ½ tsp. dried basil
- 2 cups uncooked medium egg noodles
- 1 to 2 Tbsp. lemon juice

1. In a small saucepan, saute the onion in oil and butter until tender. Add the chicken; cook and stir until chicken is lightly browned and meat is no longer pink. Add garlic; cook 1 minute longer.
2. Stir in the chicken broth, carrot, peas and basil. Bring to a boil. Reduce heat; cover and simmer for 5 minutes. Add the egg noodles. Cover and simmer until noodles are tender, 8-10 minutes. Stir in lemon juice.
1 cup: 435 cal., 23g fat (6g sat. fat), 83mg chol., 949mg sod., 38g carb. (7g sugars, 4g fiber), 21g pro.

Vermicelli Beef Stew

I love trying out new recipes, not only for my husband and myself but also for friends and relatives. Beef stew with long, thin vermicelli pasta was a dish that went over big.
—*Sharon Delaney-Chronis, South Milwaukee, WI*

Prep: 20 min. • **Cook:** 8½ hours
Makes: 8 servings

- 1½ lbs. beef stew meat, cut into 1-in. cubes
- 1 medium onion, chopped
- 2 Tbsp. canola oil
- 3 cups water
- 1 can (14½ oz.) diced tomatoes
- 1 pkg. (16 oz.) frozen mixed vegetables, thawed
- 1 Tbsp. dried basil
- 1 tsp. salt
- 1 tsp. dried oregano
- 6 oz. uncooked vermicelli, broken into 2-in. pieces
- ¼ cup grated Parmesan cheese

1. In a large skillet, brown meat and onion in oil; drain. Transfer to a 5-qt. slow cooker. Stir in water, tomatoes, mixed vegetables, basil, salt and oregano. Cover and cook on low for 8-10 hours or until meat and vegetables are tender.
2. Stir in the vermicelli. Cover and cook for 30 minutes or until pasta is tender. Sprinkle with cheese.
1 cup: 294 cal., 10g fat (3g sat. fat), 55mg chol., 455mg sod., 28g carb. (5g sugars, 5g fiber), 22g pro. **Diabetic exchanges:** 2 lean meat, 2 vegetable, 1 starch, 1 fat.

VERMICELLI BEEF STEW

RED CURRY CARROT SOUP

One-Pot Spinach Beef Soup

My idea of the perfect weeknight dinner is a beefy meal that simmers in one big pot. Grate some Parmesan and pass the saltines!
—*Julie Davis, Jacksonville, FL*

Takes: 30 min. • **Makes:** 8 servings

- 1 lb. ground beef
- 3 garlic cloves, minced
- 2 cartons (32 oz. each) reduced-sodium beef broth
- 2 cans (14½ oz. each) diced tomatoes with green pepper, celery and onion, undrained
- 1 tsp. dried basil
- ½ tsp. pepper
- ½ tsp. dried oregano
- ¼ tsp. salt
- 3 cups uncooked bow tie pasta
- 4 cups fresh spinach, coarsely chopped
  Grated Parmesan cheese

1. In a 6-qt. stockpot, cook the ground beef and garlic over medium heat until beef is no longer pink, breaking up beef into crumbles, 6-8 minutes; drain. Stir in broth, tomatoes and seasonings; bring to a boil. Stir in pasta; return to a boil. Cook, uncovered, until pasta is tender, 7-9 minutes.
2. Stir in the spinach until wilted. Sprinkle servings with cheese.
1⅓ cups: 258 cal., 7g fat (3g sat. fat), 40mg chol., 909mg sod., 30g carb. (8g sugars, 3g fiber), 17g pro.

Red Curry Carrot Soup

With its interesting mix of colors, textures and flavors, this spicy medley is something special. The meatballs make it substantial enough to serve as a light entree.
—*Dilnaz Heckman, Buckley, WA*

Prep: 20 min. • **Cook:** 15 min.
Makes: 8 servings

- 5 pkg. (3 oz. each) ramen noodles
- 3 garlic cloves, minced
- 2 Tbsp. peanut oil
- 1 can (13.66 oz.) coconut milk, divided
- 2 Tbsp. red curry paste
- 1½ tsp. curry powder
- ½ tsp. ground turmeric
- 32 frozen fully cooked homestyle meatballs (½ oz. each)
- 4 cups chicken broth
- 1 medium zucchini, finely chopped
- 1 medium carrot, halved and sliced
- ¼ cup shredded cabbage
- 2 tsp. fish sauce or soy sauce
  Optional garnishes: Bean sprouts, chow mein noodles, chopped fresh basil, green onions and microgreens

1. Cook the noodles according to package directions (discard the seasoning packets or save for another use).
2. Meanwhile, in a Dutch oven, saute garlic in oil for 1 minute. Spoon ½ cup cream from the top of coconut milk and place in the pan. Add curry paste, curry powder and turmeric; cook and stir until the oil separates from the coconut milk mixture, about 5 minutes.
3. Stir in the meatballs, chicken broth, zucchini, carrot, cabbage, fish sauce and remaining coconut milk. Bring to a boil. Reduce heat; simmer, uncovered, until the carrot is tender and the meatballs are heated through, 15-20 minutes. Drain the noodles; stir into soup.
4. If desired, garnish with bean sprouts, chow mein noodles, basil, green onions and microgreens.
1¼ cups: 438 cal., 21g fat (11g sat. fat), 52mg chol., 1059mg sod., 42g carb. (3g sugars, 1g fiber), 18g pro.
Note: This recipe was tested with regular (full-fat) coconut milk. Light coconut milk contains less fat.

ASIAN LONG NOODLE SOUP

MEATBALL
ALPHABET SOUP

Asian Long Noodle Soup

This flavorful soup is perfect when you want something that is quick but also looks and tastes like a treat. Can't find long noodles? Angel hair pasta is a good substitute.
—*Carol Emerson, Aransas Pass, TX*

Takes: 30 min. • **Makes:** 6 servings

- 6 oz. uncooked Asian lo mein noodles
- 1 pork tenderloin (¾ lb.), cut into thin strips
- 2 Tbsp. soy sauce, divided
- ⅛ tsp. pepper
- 2 Tbsp. canola oil, divided
- 1½ tsp. minced fresh gingerroot
- 1 garlic clove, minced
- 1 carton (32 oz.) chicken broth
- 1 celery rib, thinly sliced
- 1 cup fresh snow peas, halved diagonally
- 1 cup coleslaw mix
- 2 green onions, sliced diagonally
  Fresh cilantro leaves, optional

1. Cook the noodles according to package directions. Drain and rinse with cold water; drain well.

2. Meanwhile, toss pork with 1 Tbsp. soy sauce and pepper. In a 6-qt. stockpot, heat 1 Tbsp. oil over medium-high heat; saute pork until lightly browned, 2-3 minutes. Remove from pot.

3. In same pot, heat the remaining oil over medium-high heat; saute ginger and garlic until fragrant, 20-30 seconds. Stir in the chicken broth and remaining soy sauce; bring to a boil. Add celery and snow peas; return to a boil. Simmer, uncovered, until crisp-tender, 2-3 minutes. Stir in pork and coleslaw mix; cook just until cabbage begins to wilt. Add the noodles; remove from heat. Top with onions and, if desired, cilantro.

1⅓ cups: 227 cal., 7g fat (1g sat. fat), 35mg chol., 1078mg sod., 23g carb. (2g sugars, 1g fiber), 16g pro.

Meatball Alphabet Soup

M is for meatballs! Chunks of ground turkey add heartiness to a family-friendly classic. It'll appeal to kids and adults alike.
—Taste of Home *Test Kitchen*

Prep: 20 min. • **Cook:** 35 min.
Makes: 9 servings

- 1 large egg, lightly beaten
- 2 Tbsp. quick-cooking oats
- 2 Tbsp. grated Parmesan cheese
- ¼ tsp. garlic powder
- ¼ tsp. Italian seasoning
- ½ lb. lean ground turkey
- 1 cup chopped onion
- 1 cup chopped celery
- 1 cup chopped carrots
- 1 cup diced peeled potatoes
- 1 Tbsp. olive oil
- 2 garlic cloves, minced
- 4 cans (14½ oz. each) reduced-sodium chicken broth
- 1 can (28 oz.) diced tomatoes, undrained
- 1 can (6 oz.) tomato paste
- ¼ cup minced fresh parsley
- 1 tsp. dried basil
- 1 tsp. dried thyme
- ¾ cup uncooked alphabet pasta

1. In a bowl, combine the first 5 ingredients. Crumble turkey over mixture and mix well. Shape into ½-in. balls. In a nonstick skillet, brown the meatballs in small batches over medium heat until no longer pink. Remove from the heat; set aside.
2. In a large saucepan or Dutch oven, saute the onion, celery, carrots and potatoes in oil for 5 minutes or until crisp-tender. Add the garlic; saute for 1 minute longer. Add broth, tomatoes, tomato paste, parsley, basil and thyme; bring to a boil. Add pasta; cook for 5-6 minutes. Reduce heat; add meatballs. Simmer, uncovered, for 15-20 minutes or until vegetables are tender.
1½ cups: 192 cal., 5g fat (1g sat. fat), 39mg chol., 742mg sod., 26g carb. (8g sugars, 4g fiber), 13g pro.

 TIP

Don't have alphabet pasta? Any small pasta will work in this soup—or simply leave out the noodles completely.

Creamy Turkey Noodle Soup

I was honored when my fireman son-in-law asked to add this recipe to their firehouse cookbook. You can do some of the prep in advance and then assemble when you're ready. Serve crusty bread on the side.
—*Carol Perkins, Washington, MO*

Takes: 30 min. • **Makes:** 8 servings

- ⅓ cup butter, cubed
- 1 medium carrot, shredded
- 1 celery rib, finely chopped
- ⅓ cup all-purpose flour
- 1 carton (32 oz.) chicken broth
- ½ cup half-and-half cream
- ½ cup 2% milk
- 1 cup uncooked kluski or other egg noodles
- 2 cups cubed cooked turkey
- 1½ cups shredded cheddar cheese
- ¼ tsp. salt
- ¼ tsp. pepper

1. In a large saucepan, heat the butter over medium-high heat; saute carrot and celery until tender, 3-5 minutes. Stir in the flour until blended; gradually add broth, cream and milk. Bring to a boil, stirring constantly; cook and stir until thickened, 1-2 minutes.
2. Stir in the noodles. Reduce heat; simmer, uncovered, until the noodles are al dente, 7-10 minutes, stirring occasionally. Add the remaining ingredients; cook and stir until the turkey is heated through and the cheese is melted.
1 cup: 285 cal., 18g fat (11g sat. fat), 92mg chol., 823mg sod., 11g carb. (2g sugars, 1g fiber), 18g pro.

SLOW-COOKED LASAGNA SOUP

Slow-Cooked Lasagna Soup

Anyone who likes Italian food is guaranteed to love this soup. It's loaded with classic lasagna ingredients.
—*Sharon Gerst, North Liberty, IA*

Prep: 35 min. • **Cook:** 5 hours + standing
Makes: 8 servings

- 1 pkg. (19½ oz.) Italian turkey sausage links, casings removed
- 1 large onion, chopped
- 2 medium carrots, chopped
- 2 cups sliced fresh mushrooms
- 3 garlic cloves, minced
- 1 carton (32 oz.) reduced-sodium chicken broth
- 2 cans (14½ oz. each) no-salt-added stewed tomatoes
- 2 cans (8 oz. each) no-salt-added tomato sauce
- 2 tsp. Italian seasoning
- 6 lasagna noodles, broken into 1-in. pieces
- 2 cups coarsely chopped fresh spinach
- 1 cup cubed or shredded part-skim mozzarella cheese

Optional: Shredded Parmesan cheese and minced fresh basil

1. In a large skillet, cook the sausage over medium-high heat, breaking into crumbles, until no longer pink, 8-10 minutes; drain. Transfer to a 5- or 6-qt. slow cooker.
2. Add onion and carrots to same skillet; cook and stir until softened, 2-4 minutes. Stir in mushrooms and garlic; cook and stir until mushrooms are softened, 2-4 minutes. Transfer to slow cooker. Stir in the chicken broth, tomatoes, tomato sauce and Italian seasoning. Cook, covered, on low until the vegetables are tender, 4-6 hours.
3. Add the noodles; cook until tender, 1 hour longer. Stir in the spinach. Remove the insert; let stand 10 minutes. Divide the mozzarella cheese among serving bowls; ladle soup over cheese. If desired, sprinkle with Parmesan cheese and basil.
1⅓ cups: 266 cal., 8g fat (3g sat. fat), 36mg chol., 725mg sod., 30g carb. (11g sugars, 5g fiber), 18g pro. **Diabetic exchanges:** 2 lean meat, 2 vegetable, 1½ starch.

Shrimp Pad Thai Soup

Pad thai is one of my favorite foods, but it's often full of calories. Here's a lighter option that has all the flavor of the traditional dish.
—*Julie Merriman, Seattle, WA*

Prep: 15 min. • **Cook:** 30 min.
Makes: 8 servings

- 1 Tbsp. sesame oil
- 2 shallots, thinly sliced
- 1 Thai chili pepper or serrano pepper, seeded and finely chopped
- 1 can (28 oz.) no-salt-added crushed tomatoes
- ¼ cup creamy peanut butter
- 2 Tbsp. reduced-sodium soy sauce or fish sauce
- 6 cups reduced-sodium chicken broth
- 1 lb. uncooked shrimp (31-40 per lb.), peeled and deveined
- 6 oz. uncooked thick rice noodles
- 1 cup bean sprouts
- 4 green onions, sliced
  Optional: Chopped peanuts and additional chopped chili pepper
  Lime wedges

1. In a 6-qt. stockpot, heat oil over medium heat. Add shallots and chili pepper; cook and stir 4-6 minutes or until tender. Stir in crushed tomatoes, peanut butter and soy sauce until blended; add broth. Bring to a boil; cook, uncovered, 15 minutes to allow flavors to blend.
2. Add the shrimp and rice noodles; cook 4-6 minutes longer or until shrimp turn pink and noodles are tender. Top each serving with bean sprouts, onions and, if desired, chopped peanuts and additional chopped chili pepper. Serve with lime wedges.

1⅓ cups: 252 cal., 7g fat (1g sat. fat), 69mg chol., 755mg sod., 31g carb. (5g sugars, 4g fiber), 17g pro. **Diabetic exchanges:** 2 lean meat, 1½ starch, 1 vegetable, 1 fat.

Couscous Meatball Soup

Small, tender couscous pasta combines with beefy homemade meatballs and more for a satisfying meal every time.
—*Jonathan Pace, San Francisco, CA*

Prep: 25 min. • **Cook:** 40 min.
Makes: 10 servings

- 1 lb. lean ground beef (90% lean)
- 2 tsp. dried basil
- 2 tsp. dried oregano
- ½ tsp. salt
- 1 large onion, finely chopped
- 2 tsp. canola oil
- 1 bunch collard greens, chopped (8 cups)
- 1 bunch kale, chopped (8 cups)
- 2 cartons (32 oz. each) vegetable stock
- 1 Tbsp. white wine vinegar
- ½ tsp. crushed red pepper flakes
- ¼ tsp. pepper
- 1 pkg. (8.8 oz.) pearl (Israeli) couscous

1. In a small bowl, combine the beef, basil, oregano and salt. Shape into ½-in. balls. In a large skillet coated with cooking spray, brown meatballs; drain. Remove meatballs and set aside.
2. In the same skillet, brown the onion in oil. Add the greens and kale; cook 6-7 minutes longer or until wilted.
3. In a Dutch oven, combine the greens mixture, meatballs, stock, vinegar, pepper flakes and pepper. Bring to a boil. Reduce heat; cover and simmer for 10 minutes. Return to a boil. Stir in couscous. Reduce heat; cover and simmer, stirring once, until couscous is tender, 10-15 minutes.

1 cup: 202 cal., 5g fat (2g sat. fat), 28mg chol., 583mg sod., 26g carb. (1g sugars, 2g fiber), 13g pro. **Diabetic exchanges:** 1½ starch, 1 lean meat, 1 vegetable.

SHRIMP PAD THAI SOUP

TERIYAKI
BEEF STEW, P. 110

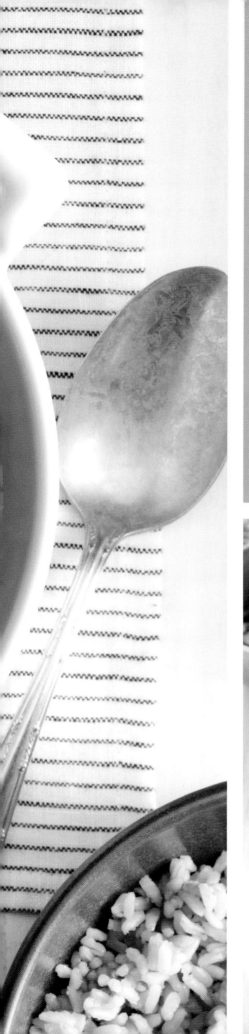

Heartiest Stews

Brimming with chunks of meat, vegetables and more, these meal-in-one dishes always satisfy.

CASABLANCA CHUTNEY
CHICKEN, P. 103

Italian Pork Stew

This delicious Italian dish makes a wholesome dinner with a salad and artisan bread. Don't skip the anchovy paste—it complements the other ingredients with a savory, salty flavor and doesn't taste fishy at all.
—Lynne German, Buford, GA

Prep: 30 min. • **Cook:** 2¼ hours
Makes: 8 servings

- ⅔ cup all-purpose flour
- 2 lbs. boneless pork loin, cut into 1-in. pieces
- 4 Tbsp. olive oil, divided
- 1 large onion, chopped
- 5 garlic cloves, crushed
- 1 can (28 oz.) diced tomatoes, undrained
- 1 cup dry red wine or beef broth
- 3 bay leaves
- 1 cinnamon stick (3 in.)
- 1 Tbsp. tomato paste
- 1 Tbsp. red wine vinegar
- 1 tsp. anchovy paste
- 1 tsp. each dried oregano, basil and sage leaves
- ½ tsp. salt
- ½ tsp. crushed red pepper flakes
- ¼ tsp. pepper
- ¼ cup minced fresh parsley
  Hot cooked bow tie pasta
  Grated Parmesan cheese

1. Place the flour in a shallow dish. Add the pork, a few pieces at a time, and turn to coat. In a Dutch oven, brown the pork in 3 Tbsp. oil in batches. Remove and keep warm.

2. In the same pan, saute onion in remaining oil until crisp-tender. Add the garlic; cook 1 minute longer. Stir in the tomatoes, wine, bay leaves, cinnamon, tomato paste, vinegar, anchovy paste, herbs, salt, pepper flakes, pepper and pork; bring to a boil.

3. Reduce the heat; cover and simmer for 1½ hours, stirring occasionally. Stir in the parsley. Cover and cook 30-40 minutes longer or until the meat is tender. Skim fat; discard the bay leaves and cinnamon stick. Serve with pasta; sprinkle with cheese.

Freeze option: Place individual portions of cooled stew in freezer containers and freeze. To use, partially thaw the stew in the refrigerator overnight. Heat through in a saucepan, stirring occasionally; add a little water if necessary.

1 cup: 256 cal., 12g fat (3g sat. fat), 59mg chol., 349mg sod., 12g carb. (4g sugars, 2g fiber), 24g pro. **Diabetic exchanges:** 3 lean meat, 1 vegetable, 1 fat.

Ancient Grain Beef Stew

For me, the perfect beef stew is comfort food with a healthy twist. Rather than use potatoes, I toss in lentils and red quinoa. Add more beef stock when reheating if the leftover stew is too thick for your taste.
—Margaret Roscoe, Keystone Heights, FL

Prep: 25 min. • **Cook:** 6 hours
Makes: 10 servings

- 2 Tbsp. olive oil
- 1 lb. beef stew meat, cut into 1-in. cubes
- 4 celery ribs with leaves, chopped
- 2 medium carrots, peeled and chopped
- 1 large onion, chopped
- 1½ cups dried lentils, rinsed
- ½ cup red quinoa, rinsed
- 5 large bay leaves
- 2 tsp. ground cumin
- 1½ tsp. salt
- 1 tsp. dried tarragon
- ½ tsp. pepper
- 2 cartons (32 oz. each) beef stock

Heat oil in a large skillet over medium heat. Add beef; brown on all sides. Transfer meat and drippings to a 5- or 6-qt. slow cooker. Stir in remaining ingredients. Cook, covered, on low until the meat is tender, 6-8 hours. Discard bay leaves.

1⅓ cups: 261 cal., 7g fat (2g sat. fat), 28mg chol., 797mg sod., 29g carb. (5g sugars, 5g fiber), 21g pro. **Diabetic exchanges:** 2 starch, 2 lean meat, ½ fat.

TIP

Quinoa is a bead-shaped grain that expands when cooked. Nutrient dense, it has more protein than any other grain. Look for quinoa near the rice in the grocery store.

ANCIENT GRAIN
BEEF STEW

MY BRAZILIAN
FEIJOADA

Casablanca Chutney Chicken

Like Indian food? You'll love this! Dried fruit and a medley of spices slowly simmer with boneless chicken thighs for an aromatic and satisfying meal. To round out the menu, serve couscous or rice.
—*Roxanne Chan, Albany, CA*

Prep: 25 min. • **Cook:** 4 hours
Makes: 4 servings

- 1   lb. boneless skinless chicken thighs, cut into ¾-in. pieces
- 1   can (14½ oz.) chicken broth
- ⅓   cup finely chopped onion
- ⅓   cup chopped sweet red pepper
- ⅓   cup chopped carrot
- ⅓   cup chopped dried apricots
- ⅓   cup chopped dried figs
- ⅓   cup golden raisins
- 2   Tbsp. orange marmalade
- 1   Tbsp. mustard seed
- 2   garlic cloves, minced
- ½   tsp. curry powder
- ¼   tsp. crushed red pepper flakes
- ¼   tsp. ground cumin
- ¼   tsp. ground cinnamon
- ¼   tsp. ground cloves
- 2   Tbsp. minced fresh parsley
- 2   Tbsp. minced fresh mint
- 1   Tbsp. lemon juice
- 4   Tbsp. chopped pistachios
     Cooked pearl (Israeli) couscous, optional

1. In a 3-qt. slow cooker, combine the first 16 ingredients. Cover and cook on low for 4 hours or until chicken is tender.
2. Stir in the parsley, mint and lemon juice; heat through. Sprinkle each serving with pistachios; if desired, serve with cooked Israeli couscous.

1 cup: 389 cal., 13g fat (3g sat. fat), 78mg chol., 567mg sod., 44g carb. (31g sugars, 6g fiber), 26g pro.

My Brazilian Feijoada

A co-worker's mom used to make traditional feijoada for him. Here's my version of that Brazilian favorite. If you prefer, replace the sausage with ham hocks or substitute lean white meat for the red meat.
—*Christiane Counts, Webster, TX*

Prep: 20 min. + soaking • **Cook:** 7 hours
Makes: 10 servings

- 8   oz. dried black beans (about 1 cup)
- 2   lbs. boneless pork shoulder butt roast, trimmed and cut into 1-in. cubes
- 3   bone-in beef short ribs (about 1½ lbs.)
- 4   bacon strips, cooked and crumbled
- 1¼ cups diced onion
- 3   garlic cloves, minced
- 1   bay leaf
- ¾   tsp. salt
- ¾   tsp. pepper
- 1½ cups chicken broth
- 1   cup water
- ½   cup beef broth
- 8   oz. smoked sausage, cut into ½-in. slices
     Orange sections
     Hot cooked rice, optional

1. Rinse and sort beans; soak according to package directions. Meanwhile, place pork roast, short ribs and bacon in a 6-qt. slow cooker. Add the onion, garlic, bay leaf and seasonings; pour chicken broth, water and beef broth over the meat. Cook, covered, on high 2 hours.
2. Stir in beans and sausage. Cook, covered, on low until the meat and beans are tender, 5-6 hours. Discard bay leaf. Remove short ribs. When cool enough to handle, remove the meat from bones; discard bones. Shred meat with 2 forks; return to the slow cooker. Top servings with orange sections. If desired, serve with hot cooked rice.

1 cup: 481 cal., 27g fat (11g sat. fat), 123mg chol., 772mg sod., 17g carb. (2g sugars, 4g fiber), 41g pro.

GROUNDNUT STEW

Jamaican-Style Beef Stew

Bring the taste of Jamaica to beef stew for a tongue-tingling twist. It's so flavorful, you won't want to stop at just one bowl!
—*James Hayes, Ridgecrest, CA*

Prep: 25 min. • **Cook:** 1¼ hours
Makes: 5 servings

- 1 Tbsp. canola oil
- 1 Tbsp. sugar
- 1½ lbs. beef top sirloin steak, cut into ¾-in. cubes
- 5 plum tomatoes, finely chopped
- 3 large carrots, cut into ½-in. slices
- 3 celery ribs, cut into ½-in. slices
- 4 green onions, chopped
- ¾ cup reduced-sodium beef broth
- ¼ cup barbecue sauce
- ¼ cup reduced-sodium soy sauce
- 2 Tbsp. steak sauce
- 1 Tbsp. garlic powder
- 1 tsp. dried thyme
- ¼ tsp. ground allspice
- ¼ tsp. pepper
- ⅛ tsp. hot pepper sauce
- 1 Tbsp. cornstarch
- 2 Tbsp. cold water
  Optional: Hot cooked rice or mashed potatoes

1. In a Dutch oven, heat canola oil over medium-high heat. Add sugar; cook and stir until lightly browned, 1 minute. Add beef and brown on all sides.

2. Stir in vegetables, broth, barbecue sauce, soy sauce, steak sauce and seasonings. Bring to a boil. Reduce the heat; cover and simmer until the meat and vegetables are tender, 1-1¼ hours.

3. Combine cornstarch and water until smooth; stir into stew. Bring to a boil; cook and stir until thickened, about 2 minutes. If desired, serve with rice or potatoes.

Freeze option: Freeze the cooled stew in freezer containers. To use, partially thaw in the refrigerator overnight. Heat through in a saucepan, stirring occasionally; add water if necessary.

1 cup: 285 cal., 9g fat (2g sat. fat), 56mg chol., 892mg sod., 18g carb. (10g sugars, 3g fiber), 32g pro.

Groundnut Stew

My Aunt Linda was a missionary in Africa for more than 40 years. She acquired quite a collection of recipes, including this one featuring lamb, pork and peanut butter.
—*Heather Ewald, Bothell, WA*

Takes: 30 min. • **Makes:** 7 servings

- 6 oz. lamb stew meat, cut into ½-in. pieces
- 6 oz. pork stew meat, cut into ½-in. pieces
- 2 Tbsp. peanut oil
- 1 large onion, cut into wedges
- 1 large green pepper, cut into wedges
- 1 cup chopped tomatoes
- 4 cups cubed eggplant
- 2 cups water
- ½ cup fresh or frozen sliced okra
- ½ cup creamy peanut butter
- 1 tsp. salt
- ½ tsp. pepper
  Hot cooked rice
  Chopped green onions, optional

1. In a large skillet, brown the meat in peanut oil; set aside. In a food processor, combine onion, green pepper and tomatoes; cover and process until blended.

2. In a large saucepan, combine eggplant, water, okra and onion mixture. Bring to a boil. Reduce heat; cook, uncovered, until vegetables are tender, 7-9 minutes.

3. Stir in creamy peanut butter, salt, pepper and browned meat. Cook, uncovered, until heated through, about 10 minutes. Serve with hot cooked rice. If desired, top with chopped green onions.

Freeze option: Freeze the cooled stew in freezer containers. To use, partially thaw in the refrigerator overnight. Heat through in a saucepan, stirring occasionally; add a little broth or water if necessary.

1 cup: 230 cal., 13g fat (3g sat. fat), 31mg chol., 470mg sod., 14g carb. (7g sugars, 4g fiber), 16g pro. **Diabetic exchanges:** 2 lean meat, 1 starch, 1 fat.

JAMAICAN-STYLE
BEEF STEW

Slow-Cooker Meatball Stew

This meatball-filled meal was a real lifesaver when I was working full-time and needed easy dinners my children would happily eat. They devoured every spoonful and liked to have a warm biscuit or roll on the side. If your kids enjoy helping in the kitchen, let them do some of the mixing, pouring or other steps of this recipe.
—*Kallee Krong-McCreery, Escondido, CA*

Prep: 20 min. • **Cook:** 6 hours
Makes: 8 servings

- 4 peeled medium potatoes, cut into ½-in. cubes
- 4 medium carrots, cut into ½-in. cubes
- 2 celery ribs, cut into ½-in. cubes
- 1 medium onion, diced
- ¼ cup frozen corn
- 1 pkg. (28 to 32 oz.) frozen fully cooked home-style meatballs
- 1½ cups ketchup
- 1½ cups water
- 1 Tbsp. white vinegar
- 1 tsp. dried basil
- Biscuits or dinner rolls, optional

In a 5-qt. slow cooker, combine potatoes, carrots, celery, onion, corn and meatballs. In a bowl, mix the ketchup, water, vinegar and basil; pour over the meatballs. Cook, covered, on low until meatballs are cooked through, 6-8 hours. If desired, serve with biscuits or dinner rolls.
1 cup: 449 cal., 26g fat (12g sat. fat), 41mg chol., 1322mg sod., 40g carb. (17g sugars, 4g fiber), 16g pro.

BRAISED
PORK STEW

Braised Pork Stew

Pork tenderloin and frozen veggies become an amazing treat when you simmer them with garlic, stone-ground mustard and thyme. A big bowlful is always a welcome sight on a cold fall or winter evening. The bonus? Preparation takes just half an hour!
—*Nella Parker, Jersey, MI*

Takes: 30 min. • **Makes:** 4 servings

- 1 lb. pork tenderloin, cut into 1-in. cubes
- ½ tsp. salt
- ½ tsp. pepper
- 5 Tbsp. all-purpose flour, divided
- 1 Tbsp. olive oil
- 16 oz. assorted frozen vegetables
- 1½ cups reduced-sodium chicken broth
- 2 garlic cloves, minced
- 2 tsp. stone-ground mustard
- 1 tsp. dried thyme
- 2 Tbsp. water

1. Sprinkle the pork with salt and pepper; add 3 Tbsp. flour and toss to coat. In a large skillet, heat oil over medium heat. Brown pork. Drain if necessary. Stir in vegetables, chicken broth, garlic, mustard and thyme. Bring to a boil. Reduce the heat; simmer, covered, until the pork and vegetables are tender, 10-15 minutes.

2. In a small bowl, mix remaining flour and water until smooth; stir into stew. Return to a boil, stirring constantly; cook and stir until thickened, 1-2 minutes.
1 cup: 250 cal., 8g fat (2g sat. fat), 64mg chol., 646mg sod., 16g carb. (3g sugars, 3g fiber), 26g pro. **Diabetic exchanges:** 3 lean meat, 1 starch, ½ fat.

Ham & Bean Stew

Yes, it's possible to make a thick, flavorful stew with only five ingredients. Simply let ham, beans, potatoes and celery cook with water in the slow cooker, then dig in.
—*Teresa D'Amato, East Granby, CT*

Prep: 5 min. • **Cook:** 7 hours
Makes: 6 servings

- 2 cans (16 oz. each) baked beans
- 2 medium potatoes, peeled and cubed
- 2 cups cubed fully cooked ham
- 1 celery rib, chopped
- ½ cup water

In a 3-qt. slow cooker, combine all the ingredients; mix well. Cover and cook on low for 7 hours or until the potatoes are tender.
1 cup: 213 cal., 5g fat (2g sat. fat), 30mg chol., 919mg sod., 29g carb. (6g sugars, 5g fiber), 14g pro.

Mainly Mushroom Beef Carbonnade

Want the ultimate in comfort food? You've found it! Hearty portobellos pair with beef for a rustic earth-and-turf combo that smells wonderful while cooking—and tastes even better. The mushrooms are so substantial and filling, you could add more of them and reduce the amount of meat.
—Susan Asanovic, Wilton, CT

Prep: 45 min. • **Bake:** 2 hours
Makes: 6 servings

- 2 Tbsp. plus 1½ tsp. canola oil, divided
- 1½ lbs. beef stew meat, cut into 1-in. cubes
- ¾ tsp. salt
- ¼ tsp. plus ⅛ tsp. pepper
- 3 medium onions, chopped
- 1¼ lbs. portobello mushrooms, stems removed, cut into ¾-in. dice
- 4 garlic cloves, minced
- 2 Tbsp. tomato paste
- ½ lb. fresh baby carrots
- 1 thick slice day-old rye bread, crumbled (about 1½ cups)
- 3 bay leaves
- 1½ tsp. dried thyme
- 1 tsp. beef bouillon granules
- 1 bottle (12 oz.) light beer or beef broth
- 1 cup water
- 1 oz. bittersweet chocolate, grated

1. Preheat oven to 325°. In an ovenproof Dutch oven, heat 2 Tbsp. canola oil over medium-high heat. Sprinkle beef with salt and pepper; brown in batches. Remove with a slotted spoon.
2. Reduce heat to medium. Add the onions to drippings; cook, stirring frequently, until dark golden brown, about 8 minutes. Stir in remaining oil; add mushrooms and garlic. Saute until mushrooms begin to brown and release their liquid. Stir in tomato paste.
3. Add the carrots, bread, bay leaves, thyme and bouillon. Add beer and water, stirring to loosen browned bits from the pan. Bring to a boil; return beef to pan.
4. Bake, covered, until the meat is tender, 2 -2¼ hours. Remove from oven; discard bay leaves. Stir in chocolate until melted.
1 cup: 333 cal., 16g fat (4g sat. fat), 71mg chol., 547mg sod., 18g carb. (7g sugars, 4g fiber), 26g pro.

Hearty Cabbage Patch Stew

I serve steaming helpings of my stew with big slices of bread. For quicker prep, substitute a coleslaw mix for the chopped cabbage.
—Karen Ann Bland, Gove, KS

Prep: 20 min. • **Cook:** 6 hours
Makes: 8 servings

- 1 lb. lean ground beef (90% lean)
- 1 cup chopped onions
- 2 celery ribs, chopped
- 11 cups coarsely chopped cabbage (about 2 lbs.)
- 2 cans (14½ oz. each) stewed tomatoes, undrained
- 1 can (15 oz.) pinto beans, rinsed and drained
- 1 can (10 oz.) diced tomatoes with green chiles, undrained
- ½ cup ketchup
- 1 to 1½ tsp. chili powder
- ½ tsp. dried oregano
- ½ tsp. pepper
- ¼ tsp. salt
  Optional: Sour cream and shredded cheddar cheese

1. In a large skillet, cook beef, onions and celery over medium heat until meat is no longer pink, breaking meat into crumbles; drain.
2. Transfer to a 5-qt. slow cooker. Stir in the cabbage, stewed tomatoes, beans, diced tomatoes, ketchup, chili powder, oregano, pepper and salt. Cover and cook on low for 6-8 hours or until cabbage is tender.
3. Serve with sour cream and shredded cheddar cheese if desired.
1½ cups: 214 cal., 5g fat (2g sat. fat), 28mg chol., 642mg sod., 29g carb. (11g sugars, 6g fiber), 16g pro. **Diabetic exchanges:** 2 lean meat, 2 vegetable, 1 starch.

MAINLY MUSHROOM BEEF CARBONNADE

HEARTY BAKED
BEEF STEW

Hearty Baked Beef Stew

Here's an easy way to make a fantastic beef stew. You don't need to brown the meat first—just combine it with the other ingredients and let it all bake in a flavorful gravy. My daughter came up with the idea for her busy family.
—*Doris Sleeth, Naples, FL*

Prep: 15 min. • **Bake:** 1¾ hours
Makes: 8 servings

- 1 can (14½ oz.) diced tomatoes, undrained
- 1 cup water
- 3 Tbsp. quick-cooking tapioca
- 2 tsp. sugar
- 1½ tsp. salt
- ½ tsp. pepper
- 2 lbs. beef stew meat, cut into 1-in. cubes
- 4 medium carrots, cut into 1-in. chunks
- 3 medium potatoes, peeled and quartered
- 2 celery ribs, cut into ¾-in. chunks
- 1 medium onion, cut into chunks
- 1 slice bread, cubed

1. In a large bowl, combine the tomatoes, water, tapioca, sugar, salt and pepper. Stir in the remaining ingredients.
2. Pour into a greased 13x9-in. or 3-qt. baking dish. Cover and bake at 375° for 1¾-2 hours or until meat and vegetables are tender. Serve in bowls.
1 cup: 300 cal., 8g fat (3g sat. fat), 70mg chol., 628mg sod., 31g carb. (7g sugars, 4g fiber), 25g pro. **Diabetic exchanges:** 3 lean meat, 2 starch.

SQUASH & LENTIL
LAMB STEW

 ❄

Squash & Lentil Lamb Stew

My family lived in New Zealand many years ago. Every Sunday, my mother prepared my father's favorite dish—lamb stew. I changed the recipe a bit to suit more modern palates, but I think it's just as delicious.
—Nancy Heishman, Las Vegas, NV

Prep: 30 min. • **Cook:** 6 hours
Makes: 8 servings

- 1 can (13.66 oz.) coconut milk
- ½ cup creamy peanut butter
- 2 Tbsp. red curry paste
- 1 Tbsp. hoisin sauce
- 1 tsp. salt
- ½ tsp. pepper
- 1 can (14½ oz.) chicken broth
- 3 tsp. olive oil, divided
- 1 lb. lamb or beef stew meat (1½-in. pieces)
- 2 small onions, chopped
- 1 Tbsp. minced fresh gingerroot
- 3 garlic cloves, minced
- 1 cup dried brown lentils, rinsed
- 4 cups cubed peeled butternut squash (about 1 lb.)
- 2 cups chopped fresh spinach
- ¼ cup minced fresh cilantro
- ¼ cup lime juice

1. In a 5- or 6-qt. slow cooker, whisk together the first 7 ingredients. In a large skillet, heat 2 tsp. oil over medium heat; brown the lamb in batches. Add to slow cooker.

2. In the same skillet, saute the onions in the remaining oil over medium heat until tender, 4-5 minutes. Add the ginger and garlic; cook and stir 1 minute. Add to the slow cooker. Stir in lentils and squash.

3. Cook, covered, on low until the meat and lentils are tender, 6-8 hours. Stir in spinach until wilted. Stir in cilantro and lime juice.

Freeze option: Freeze the cooled stew in freezer containers. To use, partially thaw in the refrigerator overnight. Heat through in a saucepan, stirring occasionally; add broth if necessary.

1¼ cups: 411 cal., 21g fat (11g sat. fat), 38mg chol., 777mg sod., 34g carb. (7g sugars, 6g fiber), 23g pro.

Turkey Biscuit Stew

This skillet dinner starts on the stovetop and finishes in the oven for golden brown biscuits on top. Keep the recipe in mind when you have leftover turkey during the holidays.
—Lori Schlecht, Wimbledon, ND

- -

Prep: 15 min. • **Bake:** 20 min.
Makes: 8 servings

- ⅓ cup chopped onion
- ¼ cup butter, cubed
- ⅓ cup all-purpose flour
- ½ tsp. salt
- ⅛ tsp. pepper
- 1 can (10½ oz.) condensed chicken broth, undiluted
- ¾ cup whole milk
- 2 cups cubed cooked turkey
- 1 cup cooked peas
- 1 cup cooked whole baby carrots
- 1 tube (16.3 oz.) refrigerated buttermilk biscuits

1. In a 10-in. ovenproof skillet, saute onion in butter until tender. Stir in flour, salt and pepper until blended. Gradually add broth and milk. Bring to a boil. Cook and stir until thickened and bubbly, about 2 minutes. Add the turkey, peas and carrots; heat through. Separate biscuits and arrange over the stew.
2. Bake at 375° until biscuits are golden brown, 20-25 minutes.

¾ cup stew with 1 biscuit: 345 cal., 15g fat (7g sat. fat), 53mg chol., 960mg sod., 36g carb. (7g sugars, 2g fiber), 18g pro.

 TIP

Have fun experimenting with herbs in this stew. When adding the chicken broth and milk to the skillet, try stirring in some dried rosemary, thyme and/or sage.

Teriyaki Beef Stew

I had a package of stew meat to use, but I couldn't decide what to do with it. Then I saw the ginger beer in our refrigerator—the rest is history! The sweet-tangy beef stew I came up with gives me a delicious new way to serve an economical cut of meat.
—Leslie Simms, Sherman Oaks, CA

- -

Prep: 20 min. • **Cook:** 6½ hours
Makes: 8 servings

- 2 lbs. beef stew meat
- 1 bottle (12 oz.) ginger beer or ginger ale
- ¼ cup teriyaki sauce
- 2 garlic cloves, minced
- 2 Tbsp. sesame seeds
- 2 Tbsp. cornstarch
- 2 Tbsp. cold water
- 2 cups frozen peas, thawed
  Hot cooked rice, optional

1. In a large nonstick skillet, brown the beef in batches. Transfer to a 3-qt. slow cooker.
2. In a small bowl, combine the ginger beer, teriyaki sauce, garlic and sesame seeds; pour over the beef. Cover and cook on low for 6-8 hours or until meat is tender.
3. Combine cornstarch and cold water until smooth; gradually stir into stew. Stir in peas. Cover and cook on high for 30 minutes or until thickened. Serve with rice if desired.

1 cup: 310 cal., 12g fat (4g sat. fat), 94mg chol., 528mg sod., 17g carb. (9g sugars, 2g fiber), 33g pro. **Diabetic exchanges:** 4 lean meat, 1 starch.

TERIYAKI BEEF STEW

BARLEY RISOTTO &
BEEF STROGANOFF

Barley Risotto & Beef Stroganoff

When I was longing for my Russian grandma's barley porridge and beef stroganoff, I hit on an idea to combine those two into one new favorite. Cook the barley using the risotto method to keep the grains whole and chewy.
—Tatiana Kireeva, New York, NY

Prep: 25 min. + marinating • Cook: 45 min.
Makes: 4 servings

- 1 beef top sirloin steak (1 lb.), cut into 1-in. cubes
- 3 Tbsp. Cognac or brandy
- 3 Tbsp. butter, divided
- 1 Tbsp. all-purpose flour
- 2 cups chicken stock
- 1 tsp. Dijon mustard
- 1 medium beefsteak tomato
- 1 tsp. coarsely ground pepper
- ¼ tsp. salt
- 2 Tbsp. sour cream
- 1 medium onion, sliced

BARLEY RISOTTO
- 5 cups water
- 1 medium onion, finely chopped
- ½ tsp. salt
- 1 Tbsp. white wine, optional
- 1 cup medium pearl barley
- 2 Tbsp. minced fresh parsley

1. In a shallow dish, toss beef with Cognac. Refrigerate, covered, 2 hours. In a small saucepan, melt 1 Tbsp. butter over medium heat. Stir in the flour until smooth; gradually whisk in chicken stock and mustard. Bring to a boil, stirring constantly; cook and stir until thickened, 3-5 minutes. Reduce heat; simmer, uncovered, 5 minutes.
2. Meanwhile, cut tomato into thick strips. In a large skillet over medium-low heat, cook tomato until softened, 3-5 minutes. Stir into mustard sauce; add coarsely ground pepper and salt. Stir in sour cream.
3. In same skillet, melt 1 Tbsp. butter over medium-high heat. Drain beef, discarding marinade, and pat beef dry. Add the sliced onion and beef to pan; cook and stir until onion is softened and meat is no longer pink, 6-8 minutes. Add the mustard sauce; reduce heat to low and simmer, uncovered, until thickened, about 15 minutes. Keep warm until serving.
4. For risotto, bring water to a boil in a large saucepan. Reduce heat to maintain simmer. In another large saucepan, melt remaining butter over medium heat. Add the chopped onion, salt and, if desired, white wine. Cook and stir until liquid evaporates. Add barley; toast in pan.
5. Stir the hot water into the barley 1 cup at a time, waiting until the liquid has almost absorbed before adding more. Cook until the barley is softened but still slightly chewy, 15-20 minutes; stir in minced parsley. Serve immediately with beef.

4 oz. cooked steak with 1 cup barley: 463 cal., 15g fat (8g sat. fat), 74mg chol., 859mg sod., 48g carb. (4g sugars, 9g fiber), 33g pro.

Creamy Bratwurst Stew

Here's the best comfort food I've ever had on a cold winter day. I adapted the original dish so I could make it in my slow cooker.
—Susan Holmes, Germantown, WI

Prep: 20 min. • Cook: 6½ hours
Makes: 8 servings

- 1¾ lbs. potatoes (about 4 medium), peeled and cubed
- 2 medium carrots, chopped
- 2 celery ribs, chopped
- 1 medium onion, chopped
- 1 medium green pepper, chopped
- 2 lbs. uncooked bratwurst links
- ½ cup chicken broth
- 1 tsp. salt
- 1 tsp. dried basil
- ½ tsp. pepper
- 2 cups half-and-half cream
- 1 Tbsp. cornstarch
- 3 Tbsp. cold water

1. Place first 5 ingredients in a 5-qt. slow cooker; toss to combine. Top with the bratwurst. Mix the broth and seasonings; pour over top.
2. Cook, covered, on low until the sausage is cooked through and the vegetables are tender, 6-7 hours. Remove sausages from the slow cooker; cut into 1-in. slices. Return sausages to potato mixture; stir in cream.
3. Mix cornstarch and water until smooth; stir into stew. Cook, covered, on high until thickened, about 30 minutes.

1 cup: 544 cal., 39g fat (15g sat. fat), 114mg chol., 1367mg sod., 25g carb. (5g sugars, 2g fiber), 19g pro.

Recipe Index